RESTING WARRIOR

A MEMOIR OF GRIEF, SURVIVAL, AND BECOMING

RUTHIE CHAMICHIAN-SMITH

the three
tomatoes
The Three Tomatoes Publishing

Published: February 2026
Paperback ISBN: 979-8-9947313-4-5
Hardcover ISBN: 979-8-9947313-5-2
Library of Congress Number: 2026903267

For information address:
The Three Tomatoes Book Publishing 6 Soundview Rd.
Glen Cove, NY 11542
Cover photography and author photo: www.flyingdress.photo
Cover and interior design: nycartdirector.com

This is a work of nonfiction. Some names and identifying details have been changed to protect the privacy of individuals. The events described are based on the author's recollections and interpretations.

This book is intended to provide helpful and informative material on the subjects addressed. It is not meant to replace the advice or services of healthcare professionals. The author and publisher specifically disclaim any responsibility for any liability, loss, or risk, personal or otherwise, which is incurred as a consequence, directly or indirectly, of the use and application of any of the contents of this book.

To my daughter, Lauren

My fellow warrior –
My light in the darkest days –
And my reason to keep going

TABLE OF CONTENTS

INTRODUCTION

For as long as I can remember, I've been learning, growing, and reaching for who I really am beneath the surface. It's been a challenge, but it changed when I began writing. Poetry unlocked a part of me I didn't even know was there. The words poured out, carrying the stories I had lived through – some painful, some beautiful, all of them asking to be seen and heard.

When I stepped back and looked at my life with objectivity, not judgment, I realized that these stories held something valuable: tools, hope, and a quiet strength I wish someone had shown me when I needed it the most. The battle I was fighting has been fought by many others before me, and it will continue to be waged by others long after I'm gone. When we find ourselves on the battlefield of life, it feels like we're alone and defenseless, without a sword or shield, without any way to protect our hearts, our minds, and our bodies from the arrows that are thrust at us.

I've seen that other people, especially women of my generation, share a similar DNA. We were taught that if we were good enough, if we were perfect enough, we would be loved. We were told to be quiet and just look pretty. We were expected to be seen but not heard. While our mothers baked Betty Crocker cakes, we used our Easy-Bake ovens, practicing for a future that was supposed to be simple and sweet. But we were cast into roles we never auditioned for, roles we didn't choose, and we were expected to perform without question. Little boys were told to "be a man" when they were disappointed or bullied. Girls weren't given the tools to identify, express our feelings, or label them so we could work through them. When the reality didn't match the cookie-cutter promises we were given (how could they?), we were left questioning our very existence. Who am I outside of the roles I've played?

It's comforting to understand that the ones who marched through this fire before us faced the storms, endured the wounds, and yet somehow emerged not only surviving, but thriving. That knowledge brings hope and resilience.

I have been walking, running, and sometimes crawling along this road for a long time. There have been a lot of obstructions along the way: early childhood trauma, the sting of relentless bullying, the disappearance and murder of my best friend, the long, brutal battle as I watched my husband of 37 years fight a 15-year war with cancer. As I watched him change physically and emotionally over several years, I had to change too. I had to adapt to and navigate our changing life.

My poem, "Resting Warrior," was born from an epiphany: When my husband died, so did I. My role as constant caregiver was gone, and I felt lost, unsure of where to go without that identity. I had also taken on the exhausting job of caretaking a difficult mother, the loss of my father, and two encounters with breast cancer, culminating in a full double mastectomy.

For most of my life, I had identified as an extension of someone else. First, it was my mother, and then it was my husband. I was always fulfilling someone else's demands and expectations, and it became clear to me that I had better figure out who *Ruthie* truly is.

Over three decades, I have learned through therapy and inner work that no matter how difficult the challenges, transformation is possible. As I began my writing journey, I found myself connecting the dots between the person I used to be and the one I was becoming. Each trial shaped and changed me. When I was thirty-six years old and my friend disappeared, that set me up for a future of resilience. While I was going through it, I didn't realize that I was polishing the facets of a rough diamond. The disappearance of a friend was one facet. Discovering her murder was another. Facing a cancer diagnosis was yet another. And so it continued with lows and highs, with heartbreaks and breakthroughs. And along the way, I observed the people who stayed with me and those who proved to be fair-weather companions.

Through journaling, I discovered that my poetry was fueled by the stories that inspired it. Therapy helped me see how these stories are connected, each thread being a stage of metamorphosis. When it comes down to it, I see journaling as our most authentic self speaking. It is who we are. It helps us name and label our feelings. As parents, we often tell an upset child to use their words. But how often do we take our own advice? When we put pen to paper, we allow ourselves to find the right words to describe our feelings. That results in clarity, one of the first steps toward healing. It doesn't matter where you start. Just start and let the process take on a life of its own.

Between the poems in this book, I've given glimpses into their back stories. They express a full range of emotions. My poetry helped me see the person that I became, not in spite of my challenges, but because of them. Some you may relate to right now. Others may resonate with you at another time in your journey. Just remember that wherever you are today, if you're broken, mending, or emerging, each of my poems can be a resting place to remember your own stories. Retrospection can help us see how the decisions we made brought us closer to ourselves, and the ones we didn't make also shaped us.

Recently, I was in my oncologist's waiting room for a checkup when I saw a woman who was having a chemotherapy infusion. Her head was wrapped in a scarf, and she was walking the tightrope of life and death. I saw her as a warrior. She made me grateful for the life I have and for my health. My oncologist said to me, "You always have such a happy and positive spirit." I believe that the way we view things from morning to night impacts us, so if we're looking for things to be grateful for and for answered prayers, we can find them.

I remember being a little girl in Inglewood, watching black caterpillars inch across the leaves of our neighbor's backyard tree. The leaves bled a white, milky sap where the caterpillars had nibbled. They were strange, sticky, and alive. I didn't know it, but I was watching transformation in slow motion.

3

As the caterpillar grew, it shed its skin numerous times. Each time, it had to split open just enough to keep going. It didn't look like transformation. It looked like survival. This stage was about consumption, preparation, and gathering strength for the transformation ahead. From time to time, I would gently nudge a caterpillar onto a stick, its tiny legs clinging as if it already trusted me. I'd carefully transport it into a "home" of my own making, a glass jar filled with twigs, soft leaves, and plenty of holes punched into the lid to let the air come in.

I don't remember what happened next, whether it spun its silken thread in daylight or waited for the stillness of night to begin its hidden work. What I do know is that one day, the caterpillar was gone, and, in its place, a pale cocoon was suspended like a question mark among the twigs.

And then nothing. No sound. No movement. No signs of life. Just stillness, day after day. I couldn't see inside, and I didn't know what was happening. Was it sleeping? Struggling? Becoming? I only knew that something important was taking place behind a veil I couldn't lift. I learned that transformation doesn't begin with flight. It begins with a breaking down. Inside the chrysalis, the Caterpillar dissolves. It is unrecognizable at first as soft tissue gives way and its former shape loses all definition. This is the stage of confinement, of stillness so deep, it feels like disappearance. The world may think nothing is happening, but inside, everything is shifting.

I related to that journey. There were seasons in my life when I felt suspended, no longer who I was, and not yet who I would become. I was grieving, questioning, unraveling. And yet, even in the dark, there was a flicker of light. A spark of breath. The earliest whispers of something new, pressing against the shell of what had been. For me, this was not my end. It was the sacred pause before becoming.

Even after it has become a butterfly, the transformation isn't complete. It has to fight to be free. The butterfly pushes. It strains. It struggles. Without struggle, the wings would remain weak, unable to hold the weight of flight. Finally, the butterfly is free. The warrior has laid down her armor.

I learned that becoming isn't just about beauty. It's about effort. About pain. About pulling oneself out of what once felt like safety, but it had become too small. The quiet didn't mean that I was finished. It meant that I was ready to begin again. I stepped forward, still tender, still uncertain, but with wings that remembered the struggle and a strength that could no longer be denied.

These acts of courage say,

I'm still here.

I still want joy.

I still believe in love.

This final stage, this season of me, is not selfish or small but unapologetically, radiantly empowered. I have found the freedom to be me, to hope again, and to love myself and others. This is the stage where I no longer have to ask permission to shine. Rather, I stand in the fullness of who I've become and whisper to the girl I once was:

"Look at us now."

For those who are living in what feels like an internal hell, desperate for a glimmer of hope, I want you to know that there is something on the other side. I've found it because I was willing to see it. I am offering a reminder that even in grief and trauma, hope is there. You won't emerge as the same person you once were, but you will emerge. And you will come to love the person you are becoming.

The following is a collection of truths that I am offering. I hope my poems bring you fortitude and comfort as you lean into your trials. If the lessons I've pieced together through therapy, coaching, retreats, and journaling can help even one person, I will have done my job.

You are cordially invited into my world.

AN INVITATION

You are invited to take a front row seat
In the intimate spaces of my mind

My heart is on the page
Line by line
You'll discover
What I've only just uncovered

A girl once lost, forlorn
Feeling deeply without words
Never allowed to be heard

It took time but she learned
Her words have power
And once expressed
They fill the void of her nothingness

So please take a front row seat
In the intimate spaces of my mind
Maybe you'll find
That we share thoughts of a similar kind

Part 1

CATERPILLAR

THE DAY MY CHILDHOOD DIED

Before I understood words like "responsibility" or "expectation," I knew what it meant to belong to something larger than myself. I was one of thirteen grandchildren, all orbiting around my maternal grandmother like planets around the sun. She lived in an apartment above our family market on La Brea Avenue in Inglewood, California. It had been in operation since the early 1920s, and it was the heart of everything. The whole family worked there, they were raised there, and that was where I spent most of my time, learning what it meant to be useful.

Beyond the market's glass doors, the city was pulsing with life. A Lincoln Mercury dealership was across the street, and a toy store, Ruby's Toyland, was a few doors down, its shelves lined with treasures. Beside it was a tire shop, and the air was so thick with the acrid scent of tar and rubber, I held my breath when I passed by.

Next came a Frosty Freeze, where we got chocolate-dipped soft serve ice cream cones on Saturdays.

A few times a year, I was allowed to visit the toy store and pick something out. When I was four years old in 1960, I got my first Barbie doll there after a dentist removed an abscessed tooth with a pair of pliers. Whenever we got a toy, Saul, the shop owner, wrapped it in bright, rainbow-colored paper. Instead of ribbons, he taped a striped candy stick to the top of the package.

Behind the check stand, there was a wall of black cat clocks, their tails swaying like pendulums, their eyes darting back and forth as if they were watching me.

Saul, whom we affectionately called Uncle Saul, would stop by our market sometimes for a visit. He looked me straight in the eyes and said,

"Hello." He was never in a hurry. "You're so sweet," he would say to me. "You're going to look just like Gina Lollobrigida when you grow up." I didn't know who she was, but I believed him.

Above, on the second floor, was my grandmother's home. The living room windows overlooked the busy street below, and I sat on my knees at the back of the sofa to see out the windows, while my older cousin taught me the make and model of each car. He pointed out Fords, Chevrolets, and Buicks from the fifties and sixties. I paid close attention to him. He teased me a lot, but he also had a creative, generous side. He loved to play the piano while I danced, twirling and singing and moving in time to the music.

There was a toy room in my grandmother's house at the top of a staircase, a whimsical place where my cousins and I would jump on the bed so hard, the mattress would slide off onto the floor. That was where my cousin built me a fashion house from a discarded cardboard box. He named it "Lucy Gallant," a name I didn't understand, but I adored that house. My Barbie doll had a home, a grand fashion house where I could lose myself in make-believe.

On the nights I stayed over at my grandmother's house, the neon glow of the Talley's drugstore sign was my night light. The sign at the corner of La Brea and Arbor Vitae spun slowly, its lights reflecting against the walls of the room. I watched it turn, round and round until I fell asleep.

LESSONS IN SILENCE

At three years old, I became disillusioned about life. I was cradling my Thumbelina doll. She was my favorite. She had a dial on her back that made her squirm, and I was playing with her when my eleven-year-old cousin, Rosalie, grabbed the doll from me, held it in front of my face, and twisted the dial until it snapped.

"SHUT UP!" I screamed. That was the worst thing I could think to say. In a moment, I heard footsteps coming up the stairs. It was my mother. She grabbed my ear, dragged me to the bathroom, put soap on her index and middle finger, and shoved them into my mouth. I became hysterical while my cousin stood in the doorway, laughing. I wanted to tell my mother what had really happened, but I realized that speaking up would only bring more punishment. I swallowed my words and the soap, and I made a silent vow to myself: "You're not going to cry today."

Whenever Rosalie and her brother made me break down, it gave them ammunition.

"Look at her," they'd sneer. "Bette Davis crocodile tears." Their bullying created trauma for me as I taught myself to laugh instead of cry. Today, I know that the teasing wasn't random cruelty. It was a reflection of their own pain. Their father had been an abusive man who nearly killed their mother twice. My cousins had learned to survive the violence by turning their pain outward, and I was an easy target.

Not long after the Thumbelina incident, Dewey appeared. He was my imaginary friend, my confidant, my protector, my witness who saw me when no one else did. When I spoke, he listened. When I was hurt, he understood, and he soothed me. My parents were confused when I refused to let anyone sit beside me. "No," I said. "Dewey sits there. You can't sit on Dewey!"

My mother had little patience for this. An imaginary friend? Something had to be wrong with me. She took me to the doctor. She was afraid he'd say I was ill, but instead, he reassured her. "Don't worry," he said. "It's just a sign of a healthy imagination."

But she did worry. Being an only child meant I didn't have the buffer my cousins had. They had siblings to take the pressure off. My mother's helicopter parenting was an ever-present force, circling and smothering. Dewey became my refuge.

One day, Dewey told me it was time for him to go home. I missed him terribly. Shortly after that, when we were on a road trip, driving on the Ventura freeway from Los Angeles to the Bay Area, I saw a roadside stand with the name "Dewey's Hamburgers." When I was sure that Dewey had found his way home, I felt safe enough to let him go.

I loved school, and school loved me. I was quiet, compliant, eager to please, and always at the top of my class. An avid learner, my teachers valued me. School became my oasis, my escape. Mrs. Hamlin, my fourth and fifth-grade teacher, noticed me. She didn't just see a well-behaved student. She saw a mind that wasn't being used enough. One day she had me tested and I was allowed to skip a year and go from fifth to sixth grade. It was the first time someone had advocated for me, and the impact stayed with me for the rest of my life.

BORN A MOTHER

My mother wasn't evil. That's important for me to say. She was shaped by expectations, and she wasn't allowed to choose anything for herself. She grew up in that apartment above the market, a member of a family where obligation was a birthright. A child of the depression, my mother was a child herself when she became a mother. At eight years of age, she had to care for her newborn baby brother while her own mother ran the store. She never had the luxury of being soft and at ease. She had never had a childhood, and as a result, neither did I.

As a child, the family expected me to work in the market. I was their extra pair of hands. I learned to count money before I started school. I knew how to wrap meat for the butcher department by the time I was twelve. I learned how to log inventory and stack a six-pack of bottles for refunds, always under the watchful eye of my mother, her sister, and three uncles, making sure I carried my weight.

For decades, I lived as an extension of others. First, it was my mother, and then it was my late husband. I was the person they needed, and it took years of therapy to find my own voice. I had to peel back layers of generational walls to see how deeply silence had been ingrained in my psyche. Today, I don't need permission to choose my own path. I just do it. I'm not the three-year-old girl anymore. I have found my voice, not in defiance, but in freedom. I embrace the little girl inside of me, the one who still wants soft serve ice cream dipped in chocolate, the one who was elated to pick out a new Barbie doll, the one who needed to be safe, protected, and free.

WINGS

My wings were clipped before I could fly
To soar up and out, to navigate the sky
I blindly obeyed
Without knowing why
Reasons weren't needed
In order to get by

I didn't learn to think for myself
I was told what to do, what to hear, what to wear

No wonder I conjured my friend who showed me he cared

He sat by me, playing the role of savior and companion
He laughed at my jokes
And treated me with compassion

Until I could unlock the door of my cage with abandon

It was scary out there in the unfamiliar sky
Especially in winter when the sun became shy
But days unfolded and warmth came to me
Through the care of strangers
Who treated me kindly

The people in my world weren't there, though I tried
They threw rocks at the cage
And laughed when I cried

Crocodile tears and soap in my mouth
Pushed me down, made me drown
Held me down for the count

Where were they, the ones who were supposed to protect?

Ohhh now I see that as long as the bird
Spent the night in her cage
They could sleep
As long as silent was her rage

Good girls don't get mad
Or sullen or cross
We smile and laugh but at
Such a high cost

I was told what to do from morning's first yawn
Fetching coffee for the Guard in the preschool dawn
She told me that I was an extension of her
She said it with pride, yes even grandeur

I was her little prized bird
At her beck and call
On display to be seen
Reflecting her mirror for one and for all

Her shadow, her glory, I clung to her skirt
But I still fell down
With a blistering hurt

In time I learned to stand on my own
A sweet little girl with dreams still unknown

Until I learned to fly with those clipped wings
Going a little farther each time I ventured to bring
My truth to the fore to meet the world
Yes, this little bird managed to climb
Thru life's branches one at a time

She saw that the world was a beautiful place
With new sights to offer and treats ready to taste

It does not belong to someone to take our free will
The gift God gave to us all, that gift He gives still

No tears can I shed
For mourning her death
They were all spent thru the years
Between my deep breaths

That Guard is now gone, so I could finally escape
And can savor my freedom as I turn that sad page

I can manage to fly to each branch on the tree
And finally discover what it's like to be Me

BRONZING THE FINGER

few months after I was newly widowed, I was living in my mother's house as her caretaker. By then, she was well into her nineties, but her mind hadn't dulled, and neither had the way she wielded her authority. She held court at the oval dining table. The L-shaped brown vinyl tuck and roll seating wrapped around the corner of the room, much like the old-fashioned restaurant booths from the fifties and sixties. That was the most comfortable spot in the house, and it became the gathering place for meals, conversations, and her never-ending lectures.

The inner Sanctum

One afternoon, she launched into a familiar diatribe. Her finger wagged in my direction. "When you were a child," she said, "you had to obey me. I didn't need to give a reason. Children are supposed to be seen and not heard, and blindly obey their parents. That's that."

With that finger wag, all of my childhood wounds bubbled up to the surface. I glanced at our friends sitting at the table, and I sensed that they were pitying me. I felt the same humiliation I had endured all my life, the nodding and the smiling, and swallowing my words so I didn't get punished. My mother was much older now, but her script hadn't changed.

A few days later, when she started pointing again, I gently took her hands in mine. I folded her index finger back, pressed it against her palm, and said softly, "Mom, you don't look good when you scold me like that. Or when you talk about scolding me when I was young."

When I was seventeen, sitting at the airport with my cousins and aunts, waiting to board a flight to Hawaii for my high school graduation trip, my mother went at it again. Her finger stabbed the air between us, and as she scolded me, I muttered under my breath, "I swear, I'm going to bronze that finger of hers one day!"

One of my aunts heard me, and she laughed so hard she peed in her pants right there in the terminal.

She didn't stop. The habit was too ingrained, too much a part of her identity. As her memory faded, she repeated the same stories over and over again, attacking who I was.

Fast forward forty-five years. I did exactly what I said I would. I went online and found an artist on Etsy who made custom bobble heads. I ordered a miniature version of my mother, one hand on her hip, the other with her finger pointing straight ahead. I was immortalizing that finger. I ordered six bobble heads, one for my mom and one for each of her three surviving siblings, with a couple of spares. But before I handed them out, I had that wagging index finger painted bronze. I gave it to her two weeks before she passed away. For the first time in my life, I had the last word.

My mother once told me that she saw me as an extension of herself.

When I shared that information with one of my therapists, she chuckled and said, "It's not very often someone hands you their own diagnosis." Before the session I had watched one of Dr. Ramani's YouTube videos, and when Dr. Ramani described finger pointing as an identifying trait of Narcissism, a light bulb went off in my head. Finally, I was able to make peace with the anger and resentment I had toward my mother. I wasn't happy about it, but being compassionate with myself helped me feel better.

I discovered that we aren't always sad when a loved one dies because sometimes our sadness got used up while they were still alive.

FINALLY

I used to sit with my imagination
Dreaming of a quiet Place
Without the background symphony
Of criticism's cackling

Alone in my ivory tower
Decisions to make without the power

Corrected before I even made a mistake
Paying the price for sins in which I did not partake

That wagging finger in front of my face
Her only exercise was to thrill in my disgrace

Even when she was old and gray
Her face would light up when she swept my dignity away

Now, with her gone
No wonder I don't cry
Or mourn in the loss
Of "good" days gone by

Now I myself can finally choose
The path that I take, win, draw, or lose
Even a bad decision or two
Is all right by me
Finding my way with dignity

WHEEL OF FORTUNE

I've always loved words. Before I could pick up a crayon, the idea that lines and curves could form sounds fascinated me. I remember the Scrabble tiles scattered across the dining room table on Saturday nights. I was barely able to peek over the edge and see those small squares, glossy under the light. They looked like a sea of letters against the blonde Danish modern wood table.

I watched as Mom and Dad took turns. My father was linguistically brilliant, fluent in seven languages, and he won nearly every time, but always with a warm, kind smile. As I got older, I'd team up with Mom, strategizing our moves to maximize our score.

Maybe that's where my love for *Wheel of Fortune* began. After school, I'd rush home to watch it on TV. I loved seeing Chuck Woolery and Susan Stafford, predecessors of Pat Sajak and Vanna White. One afternoon in 1981, shortly after I got married, I was flipping through the channels when I found out that the show was still on the air. An ad came on inviting viewers to apply as contestants. Why not?

I sent in my application, and they called me for testing. And then . . . Crickets. After the required two-month wait, I applied again. I was surprised when the producers called that very afternoon to invite me to be a bona fide contestant on the show.

The weeks leading up to my appearance were filled with practice rounds of Hangman, roping in whomever I could find to play. It was often my husband, Mark. Finally, the big day arrived. We were told to bring three changes of clothes since they filmed four episodes in a day, and a person could win a maximum of three times.

Mark, his mom, her friend, and I piled into the car, buzzing with excitement as we drove to the Burbank studio. When we arrived, the producers led all the possible contestants into a green room overflowing with candy, Chips Ahoy, Mystic Mints, Oreos, and Costco-sized portions of sugar, all meant to keep our nerves at bay. There was no guarantee any of us would be chosen.

They called my name. Show #1. I was on and I won! That meant I could go "shopping" on the set. I had the thrilling rush of selecting prizes while the stage lights glowed around me. I had a strategy. Instead of bulky household appliances or random goods, I chose gift certificates from Tiffany's, Cartier, Gucci, and Giorgio.

For example, the Gucci gift certificate was represented on stage by three pairs of men's shoes, a $515 voucher. I could spend the voucher on anything I wanted in the store. The closest one to me was on Rodeo Drive in Beverly Hills, and I didn't want men's shoes, but somehow, in Mark's mind, those shoes were his.

We broke for a cafeteria-style meal, but I couldn't eat. When I did my second show, I won again. When they called me for my third and final show, I put on my last outfit, a light apricot dress with tiny black polka dots that was not particularly flattering, but it didn't matter because I won again. I didn't take home the car in the bonus round, but I walked away with over $14,000 in prizes.

The drive home was filled with laughter and celebration until Mark said to me, "If it weren't for me, you'd have never won."

"What do you mean?" I asked him.

"You won because I played 'Hangman' with you during the last few weeks."

I was stunned. How could I respond to that? Familiar patterns were resurfacing. It was the subtle childhood undercurrent of others taking credit for my accomplishments. I dismissed the feeling and swallowed my anger, but it haunted me for over thirty-five years. I remembered long ago when I had been sitting with my mother at the typewriter. She was transcribing my handwritten words for a school report into double-spaced, neatly marginalized, 10-point type. She looked over at me and said, "I deserve your high school diploma as much as you do."

I didn't have the nerve to ask her what she meant. I knew that she would be dismissive, so I let it slide. I was seen as an extension of my mother and my husband, and my accomplishments were only valid if they reflected well on them.

Decades later, I revisited that moment in the car with Mark. I reminded him of what he had said. He was apologetic. The first words out of his mouth were, "I was an idiot."

That may have eased the memory, but it didn't erase the hurt.

Two and a half years ago, I was in session with a coach when I told him about Mark and my mother stealing my thunder. "I don't know why," I said, "but deep down, I still feel like I'm not good enough."

He nodded and said, "Everybody has that feeling. You're not alone."

His remark was casual and offhanded, but not dismissive. It felt like the truth. Those simple words turned on a light inside me. They put a period where there had always been a question mark.

It's no wonder we women have such a hard time believing in ourselves. We were raised with images of Barbara Billingsley in "Leave it to Beaver," vacuuming the carpet in high heels and pearls.

The words, "you're not good enough," may have never been spoken, but that tacit kind of criticism and expectations spoke to me louder than shouting ever could.

Dr. Phil said, "The strain of trying to be perfect is in and of itself imperfect."

Trying to be perfect.

GOOD ENOUGH?

I am as good as I can be
Though perfect it ain't
Why are you so demanding?
After all, you're no saint

I'm not your mirror's reflection,
I think you wish you could be me
There are cracks below the surface
You're hiding desperately.

You throw rocks with all your might
At this fragile wall of glass.
Why don't you just admire me
And keep your house intact?

You want me to be perfect,
Then chastise me when I'm not
Is it to bring me down a peg,
Or just to boost you up?

I'm not your soul's extension
At your beck and call.
This timid girl woke up
Just in time before her fall

You said I wasn't good enough.
I told myself,
Oh yes, you are
I learned that I was never enough.
My heart said,
Yes, you are

Some lessons were good
When I was actually taught,
Instead of derided
And chided for naught.

You micromanaged my every expression,
As if my private thoughts
Required confession

I was your toy, your plaything,
But when I grew older,
I learned how to nurture and love
Not give the cold shoulder

The way to become the person we desire
Is by finding the truth
And not believing the liar

You said, "Not good enough,"
And you know, I believed it
For so many years
Until the day I realized
You were saying those words
To yourself in the mirror

WHERE HAS SHE BEEN ALL MY LIFE?

On January 27, 1979, my best friend Nancy and I threw a party. She managed the guest list, and I took care of everything else. Among the names on that list was Mark Smith. I had no idea that name and that night would change the course of my life.

When Mark walked into the party, I felt his presence. He was with a long-time family friend of mine, Brian, and when Mark greeted me, he kissed my hand. He turned to Brian and said, "Where has this girl been all my life?"

Brian was a wiry, opinionated kid, three years younger than me, and he always wanted to have the last word. When Mark asked him about me, Brian rolled his eyes. "Don't even try with her," he said. "Her parents are nuts."

That didn't faze Mark. I had no idea that he was only nineteen; he was so confident, he seemed older, self-assured, and completely in his element. He had John Travolta dance moves, and he swept me off my feet. He danced right into a low-hanging chandelier, and he quipped, "That knocked me out almost as much as you did."

A few weeks later, we crossed paths again at an anniversary party. This time, Mark led me off the crowded dance floor and guided me onto the walkway outside. The trees shone under the moonlight, and I was Cinderella at the ball, dancing with my Prince Charming. When the night ended, Mark kissed me on the cheek and walked me to my car. We both knew that this was the start of something special.

We continued to see each other, and when I told him I was an escrow officer, he said that he was a newly licensed Realtor®, and he had no idea what "escrow" was. He asked if I could help him. That year, as his business grew, so did mine. We began to work together, and with every transaction, I saw more and more of the man he was. He wasn't just hardworking. He was also diligent, honest, and considerate of his clients. Mark was good people.

Beginnings blossom. Mark at Disneyland.

A couple of months into our relationship, he wrote me a song called *Beginnings Blossom*. Looking back, I realize that song became the outline of our life. We shared the same faith, the same business, the same passion for music and travel. But it wasn't all smooth sailing. My parents weren't thrilled he was four years younger than I was, and our courtship had its bumps. My parents were first-generation Armenian, and I was living under their roof. They were a little bit old-fashioned, so when Mark told my father his intentions toward me, it was a very serious conversation.

My father laid down the law. He told Mark that before he gave his blessing, he needed to be making a certain amount of money, as well as having a certain amount of money in the bank.

"That's exactly my goal for this year," Mark said. "See? I have it written down right here." He pulled out a slip of paper where he had listed his goals, the very ones my father had demanded. Mark was so earnest, so genuine that my father, a man who had crossed the ocean to start a new life in a new country, knew that Mark was going to be a member of our family. He had touched my father's heart, partly because my father had once stood in Mark's shoes. When he came to this country as a young student, he was full of hopes and dreams, and he had asked my grandfather for my mother's hand in marriage.

For me, it felt like a scene out of a Dickens novel — the humble, honorable young man standing before the stern patriarch, not with riches, but with character. It was one of the first times anyone had stood up to my parents on my behalf. He was making it clear that I mattered. Mark had my back with his love and loyalty.

After that conversation, Mark picked me up and carried me to the top of the hill at the end of the street, an action that felt like a promise. Without words, he was saying that we were going to conquer mountains together. In the safety of his arms, I realized that I wasn't just loved. I was being chosen.

When we made our engagement official, my parents backed us one hundred percent. For the first time in my life, I felt my mother truly relax around me. It was as if she felt that her job as a mother was complete, that she could finally exhale, knowing that someone was there to take care of me.

On June 21, 1980, Mark and I were married.

SEEN AT LAST

The invisible child ashamed to be seen
Shushed from the start
Before awakening

Ideas dismissed
As trivial dirt
I believed those lies
With all my heart

A shrinking violet,
A wallflower,
Just part of the art

You met the caterpillar
And nurtured the cocoon
In the darkness and gloom

Days, and weeks, not overnight
Changes take time
And water and light

You saw the struggle
Of that emerging life
You stood by watching
Knowing it was my fight

My fight to win
But not so alone
Your kindness and warmth were food for my soul

With you in my life
I've transcended that time
Like a dusty aged bottle

Of very fine wine

You brought out the best
That was always there
But hidden from view
Now safe to express

A PRESENCE

Mark had a presence. When he entered a room, you felt it. He had an uncanny ability to read the pulse of the people in it and home in on one or two individuals for a deep conversation. Even at our wedding reception, when it was time to cut the cake, no one could find him. He was in a deep discussion with his cousin.

Looking back, I see that Mark was a highly sensitive person. At the time, we didn't have a label for it, but we all felt it. He had great empathy, an innate ability to listen, to show concern, and to see people. Sometimes, it was to a fault. His boundaries were so porous, he often had a compulsion to tend to the "broken birds" that crossed his path. Therapy helped him understand that he couldn't fill a bucket that had holes in it. Over time, he learned to channel his energy where it was truly appreciated.

Mark was driven. He worked hard and played hard. When our daughter, Lauren, was two, we got an annual pass to Disneyland, and we went every three weeks. He took off on Wednesdays, and he made that one day count.

Music was Mark's passion. His mother was a songwriter, and when we were first married, he and his mother took a songwriting workshop at UCLA. For the first three years of our marriage, we attended the Los Angeles Songwriters' Showcase weekly, a place where budding songwriters pitched their work to record labels and producers.

Mark's songs were picked up consistently, but they were never released. And still, he never stopped writing. It was his escape, his way of staying grounded.

Finally, one of his songs got recorded by All-4-One. It was never released, but he revelled in the validation that came with it. He continued to write songs for his entire life.

THE MARK HE LEFT BEHIND

Mark was loving. He was also honest, sometimes bluntly so. But he always came from a place of kindness. He had a huge heart, and over 600 people showed up at his memorial service. A short time ago, our long-time broker had been asked, "Who is the kindest person you've ever known?" Without hesitation, he answered, "'Mark Smith.' Every time he spoke to me, he was warm and kind, even when he was fighting battles."

That was Mark. Fierce, passionate, kind. A man who had something real to give to everyone. For the years I had the honor of loving him, I knew one thing for certain. I was never the same after he walked into that party. When he kissed my hand, he wasn't only Mark. He was the love of my life.

BUILDING A LIFE,
BRICK BY BRICK

In 1983, Mark and I took a leap together. We opened Mark IV Real Estate. At the time, it was just the two of us. I left my escrow job to work exclusively as Mark's assistant. Our office was a modest 1,200 square feet, and the empty desks seemed to be waiting for people to fill them.

In those early days, I sat at the front desk, juggling the moving pieces of our business. I answered the phones, managed Mark's real estate files, handled the bookkeeping, and kept the daily operations running smoothly while he was out in the field. Pretty soon, agents started coming in, filling those empty desks. By the time I left for maternity leave in 1986, the company had grown to eight agents. My role had quietly expanded beyond being Mark's assistant. I was also the receptionist, the office manager, the bookkeeper, and the silent force that kept everything in order. When I stepped away for maternity leave, it took four people to replace me.

Mark and I worked well together. He was the face of the business, the people person with the larger-than-life charisma that drew others in. I was the one making sure the i's were dotted and the t's were crossed, that nothing slipped through the cracks. Our lives were defined by our work, and we poured ourselves into it fully.

THE WEIGHT OF IT ALL

Mark was magnetic, and people gravitated toward him. But that kind of intensity came with a cost. Realtors, in many ways, are like doctors, always on call. One misstep in a transaction and a family could be out on the street. The pressure was relentless, and I could see the toll it took on him.

On Wednesdays, he would retreat to Santa Barbara for the day to recharge his batteries. I stayed behind, keeping the business running so that, for a brief moment, his mind could finally relax. Looking back, I don't think I ever allowed myself to do the same.

Shortly after our daughter was born, Mark was diagnosed with OCD—he was twenty-seven. Finally, there was a name for the hyperfocus, the anxiety, the weight he carried that I tried so hard to help him manage. One thing I deeply appreciated about Mark was that he never resisted help. He committed to therapy, both medical and talk therapy, and I did the same as I was learning how to navigate this newly defined reality alongside him. OCD can be debilitating, but we were fortunate to have wonderful doctors who helped us keep life in check.

Even with that support, life was hard. When it came to the division of labor, the burden of the unnoticed tasks, the ones no one thinks about when they're done but everyone notices when they're not, fell squarely on my shoulders. Keeping the house running, managing schedules, handling the details that allowed life to function smoothly; these things weren't flashy, but they were necessary.

Sometimes, there was so much pressure, I'd snap. A sharp, sarcastic word of resentment would slip out of my mouth. I'd wish that I could catch it before it landed, but spoken words don't come back. They float beyond reach.

✕

APOLOGY'S RECEIPT

The look on your face
The pools of tears in your eyes
Stabbed my heart
Between two of its beats
It stopped long enough
For me to grasp the pain
Those words once uttered
Could never be reclaimed

No matter how hard I wish
Closing my eyes
Shutting them tight
With all of my might
To take those stabbing words back
Closing them away in a sheath
Locked away, never to be
Uttered again
It is too late
Spoken in haste
A reaction without intention

I don't know who that person was
That she even appeared
To take aim and fire
At the man she revered

To rewind time
Before those words took flight
Would erase the pain
Both yours and mine

But since that is an impossible feat
Please accept my tears

As apology's receipt

THE WIND
BENEATH HIS WINGS

Mark knew how to play, and he was a great dad. He loved taking our daughter to the park and the movies. The two of them escaped into a world of fun with an ease that I envied. Work was such a dominant part of our lives that somewhere along the way, Mark and I forgot how to play together. Or maybe we never learned in the first place.

If I could do it all over again, that's what I'd change. I'd make more time for joy, for play. Most of my life, I worked, and work required effort that isn't always obvious. I recall one time we went ice-skating together, and I saw it as a metaphor for our relationship. Love can look effortless from the outside, but beneath the surface, one of us was carving deep grooves into the ice, trying to steady the balance.

That first day on the ice, when Mark lost his footing and clung onto me for dear life, I should have recognized my role in our story. It demonstrated how I held him up through the roadblocks and steadied him in strife. I don't know if he noticed and understood the weight I was carrying in an effort to keep us upright.

But then one night on a simple drive home, I saw that he did. He showed me that he knew.

It was a drizzly Wednesday night. We'd had a day at Disneyland, and Mark was driving us home on the Interstate 5. It was a seventy-mile drive, Lauren had dozed off in her car seat in the back, the radio was on, and we were listening to one great song after another. It was the first time I heard Bette Midler's soulful rendition of "The Wind Beneath My Wings." We hadn't seen the movie *Beaches* yet, and still, the lyrics hit a nerve.

I was spent. The beautiful but exhausting demands of preschool motherhood, running a house, and managing a business were taking their toll.

Running around Disneyland all day hadn't helped. As she kept singing, I was staring out the car window. The city lights were like fireworks bouncing off the droplets of rain, and tears started streaming down my cheeks. The droplets became prisms of light, blurry and three-dimensional. We became quiet.

Mark took my hand, and with the other on the steering wheel, he glanced at those prisms of light and said, "That's you... with me." That was thirty-five years ago, and I remember it as one of the most beautiful moments we ever had.

Grand gestures of appreciation are wonderful, but I also like the simple ones. I see life as a beautiful quilt, created by thousands of tiny stitches, lovingly spaced. The strong ties of a marriage. We both fell plenty of times, but we always got up together. That's what mattered most.

ICE SKATING

When we first met
And we were on the ice
Skating side by side to the tunes we loved
I should have known when you held on to me for dear life
When you lost your balance
That would be my cue as a wife

It was about me holding you up
Thru the roadblocks of our life
Keeping you from falling
When blips turned to strife

I wanted you to be there for me too
But that wouldn't happen
I was the wind
Beneath your outstretched wings
I was the force that kept you from falling into gravity
It turned out okay despite that rough start
But I was always tired from doing more than my part

Some days I wonder what greatness we could have made
If the power of two exponentially grew
Into something so strong
Like a three-strand braid

I suppose I'll never know
But in kind retrospect
We were two people
Whose worlds did connect

Though we both fell down
Numerous times

Like that first day on the ice
    We got up together
A few bruises the price
For having a partner
In this game called life

THE SISTER I NEVER HAD

I was an only child, but I had eighteen cousins. Some of them played an integral role in shaping my early years, but they weren't always kind. Often, they were marred by relentless bullying. Life got easier when I was fifteen and we moved from Los Angeles to Thousand Oaks, trading the chaos of Nana's market, the family compound, for a quieter suburb. Our home sat on half an acre with a swimming pool in the backyard.

The move freed me from my extended family, although they still visited on weekends. When they came, I was my mother's sous chef, chopping, prepping dishes, setting the table. It wasn't unusual for thirty to fifty people to be there, and my mother didn't believe in paper plates or plastic cutlery. Everything was served on real plates with silverware. Then, after a meal that had taken all week to prepare and an hour to devour, I did the dishes while my cousins roughhoused in the pool and took off four-wheeling in the nearby trails.

As hard as cleaning up was, hosting large dinner parties never fazed me. I loved bringing people together and creating an atmosphere filled with good food and laughter. My mother would bask in compliments from the guests who were delighted by her culinary skills. I have to say, she *was* an extraordinary cook. She brought family recipes to life in a way that made people feel loved. That's how my family expressed affection. Through food.

That was when I met Nancy. We clicked immediately. She was three months older than I, and we attended the same congregation and the same high school, where we shared a few classes. Shorthand was my most difficult class, but it was also my favorite. It felt like Nancy and I were learning a secret code with curved lines, dots, and strokes that looked like gibberish to anyone who didn't understand them. Nancy and I would pass notes back and forth in class in shorthand, messages that only the two of us could decipher.

One summer after high school, she went to Kansas with her sister to do volunteer work. We kept in touch the old-fashioned way through heartfelt letters. When she returned, we slipped right back into our circle of close-knit friends. We went to the movies, we shopped, and our gatherings were fun, safe, and well-chaperoned.

We were inseparable during our adolescence and into adulthood. Our friendship kept deepening. We built a foundation of shared experiences that would carry us through the years to come. She helped me throw the party where Mark and I first met. She did the guest list and arranged everything with that flawless touch. That party marked the beginning of something new for me, but Nancy was always there in the background, supporting me, cheering me on. She was the quiet architect of so many important moments in my life.

Nancy and I remained best friends after my marriage, after I became a mother. She never married, but our bond never faded. While we no longer went to parties or gatherings the way we had before, there was still a quiet steadiness between us. She was my "ride or die," and I was hers. I could call her up and say, "Nancy, I need to take a drive up the coast. Want to go to Santa Barbara for the day?" She'd be at my doorstep ten minutes later.

She threw me my bridal shower and then my baby shower, and our mothers were a lot alike. We knew they loved us, but they were… let's just say, complicated. Nancy and I shared that understanding without needing to explain it. We knew how to laugh together, but more importantly, we knew how to cry together. We knew how to listen. For twenty-one years, we were there for each other through thick and thin. We talked on the phone every morning. Mark had become a confidant for her as well, especially as she navigated a series of relationships. Nancy was stunning inside and out, but somehow, she never found the right partner to be with her.

On Wednesday, March 4, 1992, I received a phone call from Nancy's dentist, who was also a friend. "Ruthie," he asked gently, "have you talked to Nancy lately?"

I hadn't. The last time we spoke was Saturday. She told me that she was expecting friends from Australia, but since she was on a deadline, she had arranged for someone else to pick them up at the airport. We agreed to speak the following weekend. I was surprised to hear that she didn't show up at her congregation meeting on Tuesday night. That wasn't like her.

After my call from the dentist, a network of friends called. "When was the last time you spoke to Nancy?" "Did she have her cell with her?" "Did anyone hear from her?"

The family called the police. Two detectives sat down at my kitchen table and placed a tape recorder in front of me. They asked questions that I couldn't answer. They printed flyers, and she was all over the news. I hardly slept, and I was on the phone constantly. Five days later, her car was found near Malibu Creek State Park. Her boots were discovered at the creek, oddly far apart from each other, hundreds of yards from the vehicle. The detectives suspected foul play. When they looked through Nancy's things, they discovered a journal. She had jotted down notes, but it was all in shorthand.

They brought the journal to me, and decoding her words was one of the hardest and most upsetting things I'd ever done. I searched for an answer to her disappearance, but there were no clues. Her entries were mundane. No mention of an escape.

I closed the journal. She was simply gone.

A year and a half later, in November 1993, someone found her body at Point Mugu. A repairman who was working on power lines in Malibu after a fire made the heartbreaking discovery. The next week, more than a thousand people attended her memorial, and none of us were ever the same. I'll never forget the moment at her memorial when her sister Janet said with tears in her eyes, "I was holding it together until I saw her friends."

I took a grief class recently with Dr. David Kessler, who used a metaphor that struck me. He said that grief is like a river. Sometimes a tree falls into it, massive, unexpected, crashing. Other times, it's like a branch where the waters gently swirl past. My loss of Nancy was the former. It felt like the largest tree in the universe had fallen into my river, forever changing the flow of everything. I've lost other people in my life, but nothing could have prepared me for this kind of loss. People still ask me, "Did they ever find out what happened?" The answer is no. There's never been a clear resolution, just heartbreaking questions that linger to this day.

Because Nancy wasn't my blood relative, the kind of sympathy that naturally surrounded her family didn't always extend to us, her friends. We were grieving too, just as deeply, and I came to understand something important during that time. Friends also need acknowledgment because our loss is just as real as that of a blood family member.

I've learned a lot since then about how to show up for people in grief. Dr. Kessler said, "If you find yourself wondering, *'what about me?'* it means you need to spend time honoring your own grief." That's what this is. Honoring Nancy. Honoring our friendship. Honoring the part of me that died with her. The void she left behind is one that will never be filled in this lifetime.

After losing Nancy, no one in my life has held the title of "best friend." It feels like calling someone a best friend is inviting the possibility of losing them, so I keep a protective layer in my heart.

After Nancy was gone, I was moved to write, but I couldn't lift a pen to paper. I tried once. I started with a cliché, like "we finished each other's sentences." It felt hollow. Trite. I abandoned the idea. I had to accept the fact that I am now a person shaped by sorrow. But along with the devastating loss, I learned how to sit with pain, how to show up for others in their grief, and how to keep going when your heart is broken in a way that never fully heals.

Nancy's loss became the touchstone by which I measure all other traumas, losses, and challenges in my life. For me, it is the very definition of devastation, of despair, helplessness, powerlessness, and hopelessness.

This kind of loss is more than life-altering. It's identity-altering, and it rewrites everything you thought you knew about safety, friendship, and how the world works.

THE TOUCHSTONE

For decades I didn't have the words
And frankly I still don't
But perhaps a picture of sorts
Can speak for me when
Language falls short

The sequoia that fell in my river
Crashed with a thunder
Sparking the lightning in a storm blackened sky
The hailstones scattered as we looked up for the answer
Impossible to find in the smoke left behind

Powerless to stop it
Or navigate around it

Our tomorrows were ended
When tragedy appended

I can't think about the how or the why
Don't know the who,
Even the where and the when are at best, vague clues

But the what, oh the what is all that matters
Your loss is the touchstone of
How deeply grief shatters

During the time that Nancy was missing, people would say, "When she's found, you'll have *'closure'*." For a long time now, I've hated that word. I still flinch when I hear it. I believe there is no such thing. People say it because they don't know what else to say. I've come to see it not as cruelty, but as ignorance, the need to fill the silence with something. Yet to me, that word feels like a command to move on and abandon a love that will never die. This poem gives voice to what I couldn't say out loud.

CLOSURE

They say when you find her, you'll get closure.
Really? What could that mean?
Shut a door? Close a box?
Can grief be wiped clean?

People just don't know what to say.
The worst thing's happened and come your way.
They don't have a clue
For this type of pain
It's never dismissed,
Not even for a day.

Closure?
Oh, wouldn't that be nice?
As if you can leave it behind
And get on with your life.

A tsunami, fire, hurricane, and quake
May start to describe the way your heart aches.

The shock, disbelief, and questions are there,
Begging for answers,
Lost—
Just like her,
Into thin air.

Closure, in my honest, humble opinion,
Diminishes the love that was once our dominion.

It's not getting over a cold or the flu,
Or closing a book when the reading is through.

The bond that you had, you'll always carry.
Whether they are here or not,
Love never gets buried.

Part II

CHRYSALIS

WHEN THE MUSIC STOPPED

March 15, 2002. The night of the awards banquet. Mark's company was hosting the event, and he was being honored as one of the top real estate agents, not just in the company but in the entire area. At forty-two years old, with twenty-three years of experience, he had built a reputation for excellence.

We were a husband-and-wife team, working side by side to navigate the high-stakes world of real estate. With two additional associates on our team, we handled sixty to seventy-five transactions a year, balancing the delicate dance of buying and selling homes with precision and care.

Our specialty was helping buyers secure their dream homes while they still needed to sell their current ones. We were one of the trusted teams that developers in our area relied upon to handle these complex transactions, making sure no one ended up without a roof over their head, due to a small detail being overlooked.

Paperwork was my domain, a perfect fit given my background in escrow. I thrived in the background, orchestrating the details while Mark took center stage. I preferred it that way. He was the face of our team, handling negotiations and building relationships, while I was the wind beneath his wings. Together, we were a perfect team.

In early 2000, Mark's dentist noticed white patches on his tongue and suggested a biopsy. Mark brushed it off. He had chewed the side of his tongue for as long as he could remember, a habit that deep thought and OCD had only reinforced over the years. But he hated it when anyone pointed it out. For a year and a half, he dismissed the white patches as nothing more than scar tissue. But a party in February 2002 got our attention.

By then, the patches had worsened, and anything acidic or spicy scent a jolt of pain through him. That night, we played a party game. The loser had to bite into a lemon wedge. Each time Mark lost and he took his turn, he nearly dropped to his knees from the pain. It was unbearable to watch.

He had put off the inevitable long enough. He finally went to an ENT who prescribed a course of antibiotics. He took the medicine, but when he was halfway through the second round with no signs of improvement, there was no choice. He had to have a biopsy.

Mark didn't fit the typical profile of an oral cancer patient. He never smoked, used tobacco, or drank. But for as long as he could remember, he had repeatedly chewed one side of his tongue, traumatizing the same spot over and over again, a factor that, while not definitively linked to cancer, has been named as a potential contributor.

We waited eleven agonizing days for the results. They came in on the afternoon of March 15, 2002, the day of the awards banquet. Squamous cell carcinoma. Stage two. That evening was a blur. Mark stood in a room full of more than a hundred people, being honored for his achievements, while we carried the weight of the news we had just received. We didn't know what the future would hold, but during that evening, we had to pretend.

The only person we confided in was Mark's good friend and broker, Brian T. He didn't hesitate. He assured us that he would be there, no matter what. I will never forget that first hug, filled with compassion, warmth, and strength.

We saw another doctor for a second opinion. He referred us to Dr. Calcaterra at UCLA, the head of the division of head and neck cancer, and the top ENT surgeon on the West Coast. He agreed with the original diagnosis, and we made an appointment to remove the mass. The first appointment available was a month away, but miraculously, someone had just cancelled an appointment for the next day. Tuesday.

We drove straight to the radiology oncologist, Dr. Randy Scharlach. It turned out that he was young and sharp, and he took the time to explain Mark's diagnosis. Then we found out that he had trained under Dr. Calcaterra at UCLA. Mark was in good hands.

On Tuesday, we showed up at the office of the man who would determine our future. He recommended radiation, not surgery; if we went forward with the surgery, a large part of Mark's tongue would have to be removed. His speaking clearly would be nearly impossible. Mark had a deep, rich, commanding voice, and when he spoke, people listened. His singing voice was unforgettable. Whether we chose surgery or radiation, our lives as we knew them would never be the same.

We chose radiation. Mark would need over fifty treatments twice a day for three weeks, and then once a day until the course was complete. He endured the pain, but as it progressed, it became more and more excruciating. By the time he was finished, he had gone from 210 pounds to 139 pounds. He was frail and white as a sheet, barely holding on.

Our daughter was learning to drive at the time, navigating the road just as she was navigating this impossible chapter of our lives. Friends stepped in to help, welcoming her into their homes on weekends and giving her a break from the weight of it all. I gave her a project to keep her mind occupied: redecorating her bedroom. She threw herself into it, transforming her space into an inner sanctum, like "I Dream of Genie's" bottle and Phantom of the Opera. It was a world where she had control over something, at least for a little while.

After the treatments, it took Mark two months to withdraw from the Vicodin and fentanyl. The drugs that had made the pain bearable were giving him an additional battle of their own. The doctors tapered his dose every three days, but even a slow reduction couldn't erase the agony that came with it. It seemed that after the treatments ended, the impact remained. Mark always had a bottle of water by his side. His saliva glands were gone, leaving him dependent on sips of water just to speak, just to exist.

It took nearly a year for Mark to regain his strength. In the meantime, I stepped into his role in the company. With the help of our team, we kept the business moving, closing the escrows that were already in our pipeline. But while I was keeping the business afloat and wearing a brave face for our clients and everyone else, I was unraveling inside. I had pushed my own needs so far to the background, I almost forgot they existed. And then, something unexpected happened.

While Mark was still recovering from the aftereffects, some dear friends from my congregation surprised me with an extraordinary gift. It was, to this day, one of the most thoughtful, generous, and extravagant gestures anyone has ever given me – a day of pampering at the Burke Williams Spa. Not just a treatment. An entire experience. My package included an herbal soak, a full-body massage, a facial, and a luxurious hair treatment, all set in a space that reminded me of a Swiss hunting lodge. There were steam rooms, saunas, whirlpool plunges, and quiet rooms with soft lighting and serene music. Even lunch was included in a peaceful retreat within the spa, far away from the noise of the outside world.

There was just one problem: I didn't think I deserved it. I felt uncomfortable at the thought of being indulged like that. Not only did I feel unworthy, but I was also afraid that accepting such a gift would somehow expose me. Someone would see through the bathrobe and slippers and know that I wasn't the kind of woman meant for this kind of luxury.

Before the big day, I brought it up with my therapist. He looked at me kindly and said, "Ruthie, if you gave someone a gift that came from a place of genuine love, thoughtfulness, and generosity, how would you want them to respond?"

I didn't hesitate. "I'd want them to enjoy it. To appreciate it."

He nodded. "That's your job now. Your job is to let yourself receive. To allow yourself to enjoy this gift, not with guilt or apology, but with gratitude. Anything less would be unkind to the people who are giving it to you."

That conversation changed something in me. For the first time, I began to look at kindness, not from the lens of thinking I had to earn it, but from the heart of the giver, the one who offered it freely. It was a turning point— one day of pampering that began to untangle years of programming that told me I wasn't enough. The spa day didn't erase the pain or the chaos, but it shifted something in me. I let kindness in without apology as I took one small step toward myself.

Mark's tongue was saved, and little by little he regained the weight he had lost. He was in a healthier place than when he was first diagnosed, and life felt fragile and precious. We fought hard as a family, and we didn't take a single moment for granted. Each day was a gift, and we intended to cherish it.

In February 2004, we celebrated Lauren's high school graduation with a grand black and white ball. Two hundred friends and family gathered, filling the room with love, laughter, and joy. I asked the DJ to play "Dance With My Father" by Luther Vandross. As the music filled the room, I invited all the fathers to take their daughters onto the dance floor and savor the moment. The lights were low, and the mood was both festive and bittersweet.

We hadn't known if Mark would survive to see this day, let alone live to watch his daughter eventually get married, so we made a choice to create a memory. Life became about that because we knew if we didn't take the initiative, life would do it for us, and not always with kindness.

Mark was still on a liquid diet until later that summer when we celebrated our anniversary in Italy. I can still picture twilight in Saint Mark's Square, the soft glow of the evening, the music drifting from one of the many orchestras. Mark took my hand and invited me to dance. I hesitated. It wasn't in my nature to seek the spotlight, to draw attention to myself. But in that moment with him, I let go.

When the song ended and the dance was over, Mark threw his arms wide and shouted for all to hear: "I LOVE THIS WOMAN!"

I was mortified, and yet, I had never felt more cherished.

For the first time in nearly two years, Mark ate solid food again in soft, delicate bites. In Italy, even the simplest pasta dish was more than a meal. It was nourishment for the body, comfort for the soul, and a quiet victory after everything we had endured. We were finding a way out of the horror of the past two years, trying to reclaim a sense of normalcy and balance. We settled not for perfection, not for what once was, but for something quieter, simpler. Something in the present moment. We settled on being happy enough as we faced what was yet to come.

KNOCKING

The signs were there
That we refused to see
But turning away
Didn't set the truth free

The symptoms you fought
So hard to ignore
Went from tapping lightly
To breaking down the door

The die had been cast
And now it was too late
To kick out this visitor
No, we had a date

The gun had been loaded
And now it was fired
Beyond our control
Taking all it desired

There's not too terribly much you can do
Except face it head on when it comes for you

When troubled times were what we faced
We looked on high to seek His grace
We needed the wisdom from above
To help and guide us
Feeling His love

Looking to Him for direction at least
It couldn't be erased,
It had been written in ink
We'd have to ride it, untamed

But it had its own mind never heeding the reins

Our only control was in choosing the way
We'd journey ahead, come what may
And only with time could we finally see
What was once in the dark now clear as can be.

FINAL DESCENT

X-rays revealed what we feared. Necrosis of the jaw was setting in. Several more of Mark's teeth needed to be pulled before they fell out on their own. I found a dentist who specialized in treating oral cancer patients. Before Mark could receive six implants, the dentist recommended hyperbaric oxygen therapy, thirty sessions, some before the procedure and some after. Mark's oral cavity was so compromised by radiation that this was his best chance.

October 31, 2013, marked the beginning of the long final descent. Mark had prepped for the treatment to have six dental implants to support his jaw. We had assembled the best dental team in Los Angeles. Every detail had been carefully planned, with two specialists in attendance. After Mark was prepped by his team, I decided to go to lunch. The office wasn't far from Bouchon in Beverly Hills, one of my favorite places. I was seated at a table next to Jennifer Garner and her friends, enjoying my salad, quietly eavesdropping on their conversation.

I returned to the office after lunch, expecting to find Mark in the dentist's chair. Instead, I found him in the hallway in a panic.

"Ruthie, save me!" he cried.

Radiation had stolen so much from Mark: his saliva, his strength, and now, the inability to open his mouth wider than the width of a finger. This was a problem for the procedure. The older dentist had large hands, struggling to work in such a limited space. The younger specialist with thinner fingers took over where he could. It was like a scene from a horror movie, brutal and unrelenting. It felt unreal, and yet, we were living it. I thought about the infamous scene from Marathon Man. But this was not fiction. It was not a dream. It was happening to him. To us. It felt like emotional whiplash. We hadn't expected things to be pleasant, but I wasn't ready for this level of despair and hopelessness. It felt like my life was being hijacked, as if I was in the midst of a Category Five hurricane with no shelter.

The fight wasn't just against the cancer. It was against the system. We were spending tens of thousands of dollars out of pocket, unsure if insurance would reimburse us for any of it. They deemed Mark's procedures 'dental,' not 'medical,' refusing to cover the treatments that were keeping him alive. The stress was relentless. The costs and the toll on Mark's body were all too much. We had endured enough, and together, we made the decision to step back, to slow down.

We needed to move into a smaller home, not just for simplicity, but also for survival. For peace. We found a spacious townhome in a gated community close to where my mother lived. There was no yard to maintain, very little upkeep. A fresh start.

The remodel was a project I was looking forward to. Our home sold in record time and at top dollar. It was in a highly desirable neighborhood with excellent schools, and after more than fifteen years, we had made it our own. My state-of-the-art kitchen had been my pride and joy. I had hung up a custom Murano glass chandelier, speckled with gold. I'd had it custom-made during that trip to Venice in 2004. I couldn't part with it. When we moved out, it lay disassembled in a hundred pieces. That was exactly how I felt, shattered into a hundred pieces with no idea how to put them all together again.

While the townhome was being remodeled, we moved in with my mother. I was caught between two worlds, caring for Mark and my newly widowed mother in her nineties. She generously gave us her bedroom where we could spread out. I used the dining room table as a makeshift office, but what I really wanted was an escape. A break. A reset.

One afternoon, I scrolled through the *Vacations to Go* website. I stopped. Surely, this was a mistake. They were offering a six-star, luxury Western Mediterranean cruise at eighty-five percent off. I called my travel agent. She verified it and booked it on the spot. The only catch was that it was an interior cabin. No windows. I didn't care. The itinerary was a dream. We would start in Nice, then on to Monte Carlo, Corsica, Sardinia, Livorno, Amalfi, and finally, Rome.

Now I had to figure out how to get us there. Mark was fragile, and I knew a long flight would be brutal on him. I pieced together business-class tickets using points, routing us through San Francisco with Milan as our destination. The cruise was seven days, and we stretched out the trip by staying five nights in Milan, using it as a base for day trips to Portofino and Lake Como.

From Milan, we took the train to Cannes, where we'd spend a night before boarding the *Azamara Journey* in Nice. We traveled along the Italian and French Riviera, watching postcard-perfect views flash past like a living watercolor painting. We hadn't realized that we were traveling on the same day as the Monaco Grand Prix and the final day of the Cannes Film Festival. When the train stopped in Monte Carlo, it was filled with impeccably dressed men and women, buzzing from the week's festivities.

When we arrived in Cannes, red carpets draped the sidewalks, and as we checked into our hotel, Jennifer Lawrence was checking out. That night, we had dinner in a tiny café on a quiet side street. I melted into my chair. We had done it. We had navigated halfway across the world to carve out a moment of peace, to create new memories. After the year from hell, I was ready. And yet, even amid the luxury and excitement, I felt the pang of loss. I hated to admit how much I grieved our home. We built it in 1998, room by room to reflect our lives, our personalities. Selling it was the right choice, the *only* choice, given Mark's health, but I was battling logic and grief.

Remodeling the townhome helped ease the transition. So did paying off our medical bills. That's how we had so many points to travel after years of out-of-pocket costs for alternative treatments, out-of-network specialists, and an endless list of "natural" cures that had drained our finances.

I was still working. Mark, despite his fragility, still came with me to listing appointments; he was still the front man of our now streamlined team. And now, in May 2014, we were at the Mediterranean. When we boarded the *Azamara Journey* in Nice, we were handed our key card and made our way to our interior stateroom, only to find that the key didn't work. A cabin steward directed us to guest relations. My stomach twisted. Had this deal really been too good to be true?

But when the man at the desk smiled and handed me a new key, he said simply, "Enjoy your cabin."

DECK 7

As we walked down the corridor to find our room, I realized that this was no interior stateroom. I slid the key into the lock, the green light flickered, and as I pushed the door open, sunlight poured in through the sliding glass doors of a private balcony. I stood frozen in the doorway. All of it, years of stress, rushed out of me in a torrent of tears. Tears of joy. Of relief.

The exotic locales were breathtaking, and there were a few transcendent moments, the kind that pull the air from your lungs. Standing in front of Leonardo da Vinci's *Last Supper* in Milan at twilight. Watching natural light glisten off Michelangelo's *David* at the Accademia. Breathing in the salty air of Cinque Terre. Savoring salt-encrusted branzino.

Mark in Cinque Terre.

But in the end, the simplest moments lingered in my memory: the crisp ice cream cone in Lake Como, the perfect cappuccino in Sardinia, gazing at the emerald green water, and the charm of an outdoor market in Corsica.

When our journey ended, we flew back home through San Francisco. I felt renewed, but for Mark, it was more complicated. He couldn't eat solid food and when we got home, he started to live off the shakes he blended in the Vitamix.

We tried so hard to find a sense of normality again, but Mark suffered from severe TMJ, another cruel consequence of everything his body had endured. We went from specialist to specialist, searching for relief. MRIs, TENS machines, injections, bite guards. One treatment after another, each promising hope, none offering a cure.

By 2016, I had fully taken over our business. Mark could no longer shoulder the workload, so I did what needed to be done. Lauren stepped in to help, making it a family effort once again, only now the roles had shifted. Worsening symptoms led Mark to revisit the doctor. Over Thanksgiving weekend in 2016, an MRI confirmed our worst fears. There was another mass, this time at the base of his tongue, dangerously close to the carotid artery. The cancer refused to leave. It lingered at the edges of our lives, sometimes retreating just long enough to make us believe we had won, only to return, knocking at the door again.

On February 15, 2017, Mark took me out to celebrate a recent escrow I had closed. He chose the best restaurant in town, determined to make it a special evening. After scanning the menu, he realized there was only one thing he might be able to eat. French onion soup, one of his favorites. He explained his condition to the waiter, who kindly offered to have the soup blended for him, leaving out the bread and cheese. Mark was thrilled.

At first, I felt guilty when my perfectly prepared filet mignon arrived, but he looked content, savoring what he could. In that moment, the joy on his face erased my guilt. After dinner, the waiter surprised us with dessert, although I hadn't ordered any. Written in chocolate on the plate were the words: For My Top Producing Realtor! Loyal Wife! Perfect Mother!

Later, Mark spoke with the piano player at the bar, and he took my hand. We danced. Our last dance. Just the two of us, like it had been in St. Mark's Square eleven years earlier.

Looking back, I believe Mark knew that he wouldn't be with me when June 21, 2017, arrived. Our thirty-seventh anniversary. In his quiet way, he had celebrated it and made sure to give me that night, that dance, that moment.

From this vantage point in time, I realize that survival is often less about finding peace and more about learning to live with the ache of what's been lost. You adapt. You brace yourself. You stop expecting things to go your way because disappointment has worn you down too many times. And little by little, you grow callouses, not on your hands, but on your heart.

CALLOUSES ON YOUR HEART

Have you ever been awakened from a dream
By a slap across the face?
That's reality
So you'd better brace yourself

Don't dream too much,
Because dreams don't come true
Unfulfilled wishes, day after day,
Become callouses on your heart

What you once looked forward to
Is ripped away from you

Once, maybe twice-okay
But day after day,
When what you love is torn away
Form callouses on your heart

Soon you stop loving
Then you stop hoping
Then you shield what's left inside

Once, maybe twice-okay
But when your violin is smashed
And your dreams are torn away
You survive by having
Callouses on your heart

It's the only thing that stops the pain
When everything you've ever loved
Has been torn away

BETWEEN GOODBYE
AND GOODBYE

There are surprising feelings that arise when a person navigates the river of grief. Not all of them are tidy. Not all of them make sense.

Between the time Mark was first diagnosed with cancer in March 2002 and his passing on April 18, 2017, we learned to deeply appreciate the good while enduring the unthinkable. Those fifteen years trained us how to find slivers of joy in bleakness, how to celebrate the good moments. But they also placed us in a state of constant vigilance. Fifteen years of fight or flight. Fifteen years on the roller coaster that many of us know all too well.

After Mark's death, the silence was deafening, even though my caregiving role hadn't truly ended. It had simply shifted to my ninety-four-year-old mother. But the hat I wore as mom's caregiver had been designed by someone else entirely. Mark's illness was jagged, spiked with sudden pain and emergencies. I never knew when he had to stop eating solid food or he'd call out in agony, mid-sentence. Everything was urgent. Everything was unpredictable.

With Mom, it was different. She was slowing down. Her body was obeying her less and less, but she still insisted on her independence. She made her own meals. She balanced her checkbook. She tried to make sure I didn't worry. Tasks that once had taken her an hour to complete stretched into a full day. But still, she did them. I was grateful.

When I look back on October 31, 2013, the date when everything shifted, many of my memories come not from inside me but from my phone. The photos help me remember. I scroll through them and piece together what I lived through: images of blooming lemon trees, a bumper crop that was once harvested and piled high in my sink. They gave me the strange idea that maybe I would make limoncello out of the lemons that described my life.

I was living an out-of-body experience, and I knew it. I was going through the motions. If there had been an Oscar for "Best Performance of Normal," I would have won it. Tears had always been difficult for me. After Mark passed away, they were impossible. The persona I wore each day gave people around me the impression that I was healing. But I wasn't. I was still lying in the wreckage. I felt like I'd been hit by a freight train and peeled off the tracks as some kind of two-dimensional paper doll, flattened and unrecognizable.

It wasn't until much later, after the noise quieted and time had softened the edges, that the words finally came.

TEARS

Tears are hard for me to cry
Sometimes I think that the well has run dry
Too many times I drew them up
From childhood days
Where they'd interrupt

But once they are there
Without being forced
Confused, bewildered-
What is their source?

My mind turns to you when it's in this wreck
And shuffles thru feelings like cards in a deck
Is it missing the love that I felt in my heart?
Or the intense pain because we had to part?
Am I grieving lost years of good times past?
Or the hope of a future that never could last?

Remembering golden moments too few and so precious
Causes that lump in my throat
We thought time wouldn't perish

Just one do over, all right maybe two
Might ease the sobs
Of the wistful adieu

Will those tears be quiet
Long enough to find
Some peace in this riot
That lives in my mind
Peace! What I crave

And haven't quite known
Until now, serenity

When I'm all alone
No more need for sacrifices heaped up to the sky
Or the wink of approval
From a critical eye

So where do these tears come from?
What is their source?
A sad sense of relief
That their life ran its course

RELIEF

I learned from Doctor Kessler that grief from loss can activate old traumas. One loss can trigger emotions from something much earlier, and a raw anger can emerge seemingly out of nowhere. It can feel like a small bog of emotions pulling at you from different directions.

It felt like I was shuffling through feelings like a deck of cards. All I really wanted was peace. Sometimes it comes in the form of silence. Sometimes in relief. Sometimes a wave of melancholy washes over you. All of it is okay. We need to give ourselves permission to feel those feelings, whatever they are. If we can write in order to label our feelings, it helps.

I've learned that there's no right or wrong way to begin. Sometimes the simple act of putting a feeling into words opens a door we didn't even know was there. I know this because the following segment is what I wrote when prompted by Doctor Kessler and his editor, Andrea Cagan, with the question… "I am surprised by my feelings of…"

I felt something I never expected.

Relief.

Relief that my phone no longer played Adam Lambert's "What Do You Want From Me?" That was the ringtone that warned me when Mark was reaching out for me to play "steppin' and fetchin.'" My therapist used this term to describe the exhausting dynamic I'd fallen into. Always alert, always scrambling, moving from one demand to the next like a servant on standby. It wasn't just about meeting needs. It was also about the feeling that my worth was measured in how quickly I could respond.

Relief that I didn't have to race to five different stores to find the right water or the protein powder he liked or the exact brand of supplement he believed might save him.

Relief that I was no longer trapped in a one-hour window, trying to accomplish three hours' worth of tasks.

Relief that I was no longer the target of pain-induced outbursts.

Relief that the endless, expensive parade of alternative treatments had stopped.

Relief that every waking moment and most of the sleeping ones, too, no longer had to revolve around the impossible task of making someone who was dying just a little more comfortable.

The truth was that Mark was dying, but in the last years of his life, he didn't see it. For a long time, I didn't either. It was easier to stay in motion, researching the next supplement, booking the next appointment, blending the next shake. I clung to these rituals because they brought me hope, even if that hope was threadbare. We were so deep in survival mode that facing the inevitable felt like betrayal.

But the inevitable came. And when it did, I was left not only with the grief of losing Mark, but with the unraveling of a life that had revolved around him for so long. When he was gone, it wasn't only the man I lost. I lost my business partner. I lost my purpose, and that compounded the grief in ways I couldn't explain at the time.

Even my body didn't know what to do. The memory of caregiving took a while to fade. I'd catch myself listening for his voice, expecting to hear the Vitamix or the sudden call for help, forgetting, for a split second, that the world had gone quiet.

What we as a family had been through in the final months leading up to Mark's passing was unsustainable. And yet, now with him gone, the silence was also unsustainable. At Mark's burial service, I told a story about him. He hated mornings, he struggled to talk, and he didn't even drink coffee. But he'd sit with me just to chat for a little while. That was his gift to me, a quiet act of love that became my favorite time of day.

WHERE I STILL FIND YOU

I see your eyes
In my morning coffee
I hear your voice
In the make-believe morning chatter
That used to start my day
Those tiny stitches in life
That kept out the fray

I feel your caress
In the soft breeze at twilight

When you swept me to dance
Before the moon grew too bright

The support you supplied
At just the right time
Softened the harshest
Of critics' brash lines

When your eyes filled with tears
To reflect those in mine
You infused quiet strength
To my weakened spine

Now you're gone
But you've left behind
A mosaic of sorts
Of happier times

Though years have passed
Time has not eased

The longing for you
That lives within me

In grief, nothing stays the same. Our feelings are rearranging themselves. Grief is like a mosaic, but not the kind that stays fixed. It shifts. I think about sand mosaics, layers of colored sand pressed between two panes of glass, enclosed in a frame. When you twist it, side to side, up and down, you always end up with a different piece of art.

Grief feels like that. The more we fight it, the harder it becomes to accept it for what it is. The sands of our life have changed and are always changing.

One night, I had dinner with a group of my female friends. There were some widows, some divorcees, and some of them were happily married. As I ate, I found myself looking at everyone's hands. Some wore their wedding rings. Some didn't. At the time, I was struggling with the question, Do I keep wearing my wedding ring or not? So many women who lose a partner through death or divorce face this dilemma. There is so much emotional weight tethered to *the ring*.

As I fiddled with it, I reflected not only on the ring's symbolism but on all the nuanced ways Mark continued to be with me. And beneath the surface of that reflection lived another truth, one I struggled to admit out loud: I felt relief. Grief isn't always a straight line. Sometimes it's felt through regret. Sometimes it drags you back to the words you wish you could unsay.

THE RING

Whether you left me by choice or by chance
When do I take the ring off my hand?
Our promise to love 'til death us do part
Can't really be finished if I believe my heart

Sorting out the moments
Of our entwined lives
Is both bitter and sweet
At the same time

Sometimes when I try to deeply inhale
I clutch at my chest with moist hands and turn pale

You're gone, it's a fact
That I have to accept
But way deep inside
It feels like reject

This sign of unending love you placed on my finger
Is what the world sees as my memories linger

How long will they be a part of me
While I try to move on and set myself free
The fact is you're gone

Whether by choice or by chance
I have to do something to get out of this trance

Tiny but mighty
It announced that I was loved
And adored
Speaking volumes in silence
With a very loud roar

The ring, the symbol of love unending
Is the price for my ransom
From life's chapter that's pending

Is it a trophy or a relic?
It's more than a keepsake
From times more idyllic

This ring, this symbol of love unending
Is forcing me to taste bitter with sweet
While my heart is mending

I don't think that I can part with it though
It's life's souvenir and love's memento

Maybe one day, but for now I'll keep it
Tucked safely away, so I can always reach it.

IF ONLY THEY KNEW

They think they know.

When I tell people I'm a widow, I see a look of pity on their faces. Sometimes it's accompanied by a sigh or a soft, clumsy phrase like "I'm so sorry," or "That must be so hard." I've learned to smile and nod. They don't realize that I'm not a victim. I'm not a martyr. I'm not a saint. I'm just someone who lived through something impossibly hard and came out the other side different than who I was before.

I've spent the last eight years processing and peeling back the layers of a complicated thirty-six-year marriage and partnership. The realizations that emerge in grief are wildly unpredictable. They range from aching sadness to anger, from wistful longing to moments of relief and pride. Not the pride of a job well done because there is no right way of doing this. It's pride in a job done as well as possible.

I've finally emerged from the battlefield, and I wish people knew that I've changed. I'm no longer a reflection of my husband, no longer an extension of his identity. Although I miss parts of him, I'm deeply curious and excited to discover who I am without the .EXT at the end of my name.

The loss itself isn't the whole story. It was the long illness that came before, the fifteen years where our lives revolved around a cruel, unpredictable intruder named cancer. He was an uninvited houseguest with no manners, no regard. One moment he was silent and the next moment he was screaming. He'd vanish, only to return like a sinister prankster. "Oh, you think I'm gone? I'm baaaaack." He slipped past every boundary we tried to build, a ghostly ectoplasm that controlled the narrative until the day Mark finally died.

The last five years of his life were about torturous treatments. Spontaneous pain. The constant whir of the Vitamix echoing through our home, like a daily metronome of decline. I was a first-hand witness, standing by helplessly while the person I loved slowly, so slowly, lost the version of himself that he once was. But his core remained untouched, flickering beneath the surface.

WHAT'S THE WORST
THAT CAN HAPPEN?

Hiding beneath the covers,
Afraid to welcome dawn—
What's the worst that can happen
After morning's first yawn?

Don't let anxiety, so familiar,
Knock at your door.
Not today, nor tomorrow—
You've been there before.

Gaining strength takes time—
One step, one climb.
You retell the story,
Reclaim its rhyme.

The toll of life's hardships
Has already been paid.
What's the worst that can happen?
It happened yesterday.

Grant yourself permission
To move through the storm—
Each gust makes you fearless,
Resilient, reborn.

Fear is the unknown,
But you've faced it all.
Scorched, yet unburnt,
You rise from the fall.

The warrior within,

Once eager to hide,
Has won countless battles,
Fought deep inside.

No need to linger beneath the covers
Greet dawn's embrace—
A new day, another chance,
With renewed grace.

The voice of experience
Has granted your Degree
You've earned the right to be fearless,
Unfettered and free.

NOT A STRAIGHT LINE

It's not a straight line, this kind of grief.
It's a firestorm that changes who you are forever.

And when the smoke cleared, I wasn't sure who I was without the fire.

But piece by piece, I've begun to find out.

There's something I wish people could see:
The woman I am now was not born of ease.
She rose from ashes, quietly, without fanfare.
And though her armor may be softer now, she still carries the strength
of someone who knows the worst—and dares to hope anyway.

I CAN DO THIS

I can do this
Not on my own
Treading lightly
Into the unknown

Biding my time
Is yesterday's news
Now I'm ready
To live life's vivid hues

Inhaling deeply
Before taking the plunge
Closing my eyes
To old pain expunge

Rising to the surface
With an elegant grace
Like Esther Williams'
Glistening face

Building with blocks
One at a time
Have finally become
A new home that's mine.

NOT AGAIN

I was diagnosed with invasive lobular carcinoma in January 2019, just six months after my mother died and not quite two years after losing Mark. Cancer. You would think that kind of news would stop a person in her tracks, but I was already moving in so many directions: renovating my home, working, keeping myself busy, that there wasn't room to feel much.

Dr. Kristi Funk was calm, clear, and direct. "Turn on your recorder," she said before explaining everything. She didn't sugarcoat it, but she didn't sound alarmed either. She prescribed a lumpectomy and thirty rounds of radiation. She said they had caught it early, and most likely it was Stage 1.

I nodded. I said yes to everything. I wanted it out. Out of my body and out of my mind. I posted my weekly progress on Instagram, encouraging my friends to get their mammograms. I framed it all in brave warrior fashion.

What I didn't say was how surreal it all felt, like I was watching someone else go through it. The grief over Mark and the fresh ache from my mother's death was still swirling. I was emotionally threadbare.

Dr. Randy Scharlach joined my team, the very same radiation oncologist who had cared for Mark all those years ago. That full-circle moment settled me. The comfort, familiarity, and compassion that I felt from Dr. Scharlach were like one big hug.

After the treatments, I was sent to the medical oncologist to start the five-year regimen of the medication that would keep the cancer from reappearing. I stayed vigilant, and I believed that this chapter was closed.

Four years passed nearly to the day. January 2023. It was a routine mammogram. I had been there countless times since my lumpectomy, radiation, and the daily doses of Femara that were supposed to keep the cancer at bay. Stage 1, no lymph node involvement. I had done everything right. I was healthy; this was just a formality.

And there it was. I could tell something was amiss when the technician took extra screenshots of the intrusive shadows lurking where there should have been none.

"We need to do a guided needle biopsy," she said.

I heard the words, but my brain refused to process them. I had been down Cancer Road before, but this time, I wasn't posting about it. No Instagram updates. No rallying cry for early detection. Just a sinking, unbearable weight.

When the results came back, DCIS, stage zero, I told myself it wasn't as serious as last time. My head went to that dark, terrifying place anyway. Why is this happening again? I was angry. I had already fought this battle before, and I had won. And here it was again, violating my body, causing me to play a waiting game with my life.

More tests. More results. Forty percent chance of recurrence. Unacceptable. I refused to live under that looming shadow, waiting for cancer to take another shot at me. This time, I was taking control. If cancer thought it could creep back in, it was about to find out how wrong it was. I chose to take away its power. I chose to make sure there would be no next time.

Under the expert care of world-renowned breast cancer surgeon and scientist, Dr. Kristi Funk, and with the reconstructive expertise of Dr. Edward Rey at Cedars Sinai, I underwent the radical surgery that terrified me. Not so much the fear of losing my body, but the fear of leaving my daughter without a mother.

Lauren was sixteen when her father was first diagnosed with tongue cancer. She had witnessed the ravages of oral radiation and the aftereffects, and she was thirty-one when he died. Enduring that kind of loss again, watching cancer taking its slow, merciless death march through our lives, was an unacceptable price to pay. I refused to let her go through that.

The day before her birthday in March 2023, I had the surgery with the option for reconstruction. There would be more procedures to come, more healing ahead, but the dark cloud that had loomed over my head finally lifted. When Lauren asked me to join her in France in June, just before she was meeting her husband and friends there, I didn't hesitate. It would be a mother-daughter trip, a chance to celebrate life, resilience, and the love that had carried us through.

My wedding anniversary was June 21. Those landmark dates are the potholes of life, all part of the collateral damage of grief. Lauren did not want me to be alone, thousands of miles away from her on my anniversary.

Hope in Paris.

I had come to embrace a simple but profound truth. If we don't create our own memories, life creates them for us, and those memories aren't always the ones we would choose. I made it my mission to punctuate this trip with sights, smells, and sounds that would leave an indelible mark on our minds and in our hearts. I wanted us to experience every moment, to make this trip a celebration of life rather than a reminder of loss.

We decided to start our vacation in Reims, wandering through the historic champagne houses before making our way to Paris. The day that we arrived, there was a music festival, a celebration on the streets. The heart of the festivities was at our hotel, nestled across the street from the cathedral. Live music filled the air, tables overflowed with champagne, and for the first time since Mark passed away, I felt a lightness of being. Being there was lifting me beyond my grief, offering me a road map stretching out before me with a different view of my life. The bubbles that danced in my glass pulsed through my veins, infusing me with something I hadn't felt in years. Possibility.

The haze that had once clouded my vision of the future was starting to dissipate. My doctors assured me that the most recent cancer wouldn't be making another appearance, and for the first time in so long, I felt relief. Muscles that had been tense for years finally softened.

I made the choice consciously and deliberately to start over. I wanted a new chapter, one of my own making. Looking back at the photos from that trip, I see how often I was looking up toward the sky, that endless expanse, as if it were a blank canvas waiting for me to begin again.

HOPE

The bubbles of Epernay gently roused me from sleep
Tickling the hope within me buried deep

My head in the clouds of desperately seeking
A new place without you, my partner, my king

When you became absent
Taking your leave
A vacuumed soul was left to grieve
Going thru moments of motions so numb
I didn't know what I could become

I needed to make a change of scene
Shake up my surroundings to tap into me

The stage was set with you by my side
For so many years there was nowhere to hide
People would not see me without you
So I left them behind to discover something new

The transformation that then arrived on the scene
Was a new person cast into the role of me

Those beautiful bubbles in the city of Reims
Symbolized Hope in more than my dreams
At the base of the Tower in the City of Light
The sight became clear as I looked up to the sky

Now instead of my head bowed low
My gaze went upward, and my blood started to flow

Living again became more than a dream
When those bubbles of Champagne crowned its new Queen

REBIRTH

My rebirth happened in stages. First in Reims. Then in Paris. When we checked into our Parisian hotel, I made the conscious decision to leave each place or person we encountered better than when I found them.

The Guest Relations man who checked us in was exceptionally kind. Instead of just handing over our key, he personally showed us to our suite, a beautiful space overlooking the central courtyard, tucked away from the hustle and bustle of the Champs-Elysees and Avenue George V. This man's warmth set the tone for our stay, but I had no idea that my presence had left an impression on him as well. I found out at the end of the stay when I found a note he had quietly slipped inside my portfolio.

> "Dear Ms. Smith, it has been a real pleasure to receive you in here as a such special guest. Always you have been smiling. Always so elegant! People like you, Ms. Smith, make that hard job so worth it! Believe me. It is the truth! Thank you for everything.
> P.S. Please keep being so nice with others!
> P.S.2 Enjoy life: Life is too short and beautiful."

That small gesture reinforced my new attitude. I saw that the energy we put into the world has a ripple effect, often in ways we don't realize. From that moment on, no matter how I felt, I was determined to do my best to leave a positive imprint on the people I encountered each day.

The next phase of my metamorphosis unfolded one month later through a series of coincidences that were too perfect to be random. A friend was booked on an Alaskan cruise and needed a roommate. She extended the invitation to me, and I said yes. I had no idea that this spontaneous decision would set something new into motion that would change me in ways I never expected.

The first night, as we left the ship's theater after an evening show, we passed by the piano lounge where a voice stopped me in my tracks. A soul-stirring version of Cat Stevens' "Father and Son" poured into the corridor. It was either the lyrics or the way Colin, a spellbinding pianist and vocalist, performed it that captivated me. I went into the lounge and sat down. One beautiful song led into another as a familiar warmth spread through me that I hadn't noticed I was missing.

My father had been a truly gifted pianist. That night on the ship, when Colin played "Those Were the Days," it felt like I had stepped back in time. My friends and I had line danced in my house while Dad played that song. I understood what had been missing from my life. Music! Sweet, sad, loving, joyful, nostalgic, and melancholy all at once. My father played the piano every day of his life until shortly before he passed in 2009.

Music had been woven into the fabric of my life in another profound way. It was through my husband's passion for songwriting. He had been a songwriter since the age of eleven, and on our second date, he shared his lyrics with me. In that moment, I saw him, not just as the man sitting next to me, but someone with a kind and insightful heart, and a depth of feeling. I knew I could love him.

Throughout our marriage, we worked together on his lyrics, refining each line, filling the melodies with meaning. It was something I cherished. In the past five years, music had been gone, leaving behind an absence. Not until that night, in the warmth of the piano lounge, did I recognize the void.

I went back to the lounge every night for the rest of the cruise. With each song, I felt that I was crossing over from hope to reality. Music was unlocking emotions I had spent years swallowing. Grief, pain, and the fogginess of the cancer-fighting medications. I had gained fifteen pounds, and I was feeling the weight of loss and everything else I had endured.

The more I listened, the more I became aware of the artist behind the music. Colin's blend of performance, warmth, and connection made every song come alive. Experiencing his playlist was like flipping through the chapters of my life, my memories unfolding one by one. I was emerging from the darkness and rediscovering the lightness of being myself again. Hope became something more than a fragile wish. It became grounded in the familiar, something I could trust. It turned into faith, a reassurance that I was on the road back. My friend noticed how happy I was. One night, she turned to me and said, "What happened to Ruthie? I'm so glad she came back!"

Hope in Alaska.

CHORDS OF AWAKENING

You awakened me from slumber—
More brilliantly than any prince's kiss.
From years of sleep,
But not years of bliss.
Tossing and turning,
Feeling restless yearning,
Watching myself,
Wishing myself
Back into reality.

Hopeful—ever hopeful—
Of a tomorrow that would bring release.

One night it happened,
Most unexpectedly.
I wasn't looking…
But I heard it.
The music came beckoning.

A gentle pull lured me in,
The tug of chords drawing my heart—
Still cocooned in hibernation,
Waiting for its beating to start.
Melodies evoking memories,
Of years passing before my eyes,
Giving meaning to the moments
That made up my life.
There was a void—

Life had taken its toll.
But your songs made me whole.
They rewound the silence,

Softened the pain,
And started me over—
Grateful again.
The weary lines etched on my face

Tell the stories I can't erase.
But I'm not trying to.
I've run that race.

And the bridge that led me
Out of that pitiful place—
Were your chords
That drew me in
And made me feel safe.
You awakened me from slumber—

That's what you gave to me.
More brilliantly,
More gallantly,
Than any prince's kiss
Could ever be.

The transformation was undeniable, and I wanted and needed more to cement the transition I was making. The cocooned Caterpillar was flexing its wings, preparing to emerge, and I wasn't about to let that feeling slip away. Then, as if the universe had conspired to keep the momentum alive, I found out that Colin's next contract placed him on the same ship where some of my friends would be sailing just three months later, in October. I booked a cabin for myself. When I learned that one of the stops would be Santorini, an idea began to take shape.

THE KEY

What key do you have
Was it something you found
Did I lose it once upon a time
Or was it never mine

Whatever door it unlocked
And hidden room I entered
Vast riches I discovered
When I stood in its center
Hope
Joy, enthusiasm, a zest for life
Once smothered in a quagmire
Of a grief-stricken wife
Rushed in like a fire starved for air

What key do you have
What gift do you possess
Please share it with me
To ease my loneliness

The darkness of the center
Of that very black hole
Was sucking me in
With no way to console

But now that the door is open so wide
The windows light up with the morning sky
If you found that Key, then so can I
To know it exists will help me get by.

Part III

THE STRUGGLE

RESTING WARRIOR

My daughter had told me about the flying dresses of Santorini. They were breathtaking gowns that billowed dramatically in the island's golden light. I had seen Captain Kate McCue's Instagram posts featuring these stunning dresses against the backdrop of the caldera, and the imagery stayed with me.

I began to envision a photoshoot, not just for the beauty, but to capture the essence of a warrior woman. A woman I now recognized as me. The final piece fell into place when my daughter, Lauren, decided to join me. That made up the ingredients for an unforgettable experience, a moment that would become one of the highlights of my life.

Resting Warrior began as a journal entry inspired by a meme I saw on Instagram. A Warrior Woman was standing on the top of a mountain, gazing downwards. The caption read, "Some days she is a warrior. Some days she is a broken mess. Most days, she is a bit of both. But every day she is there. Standing. Fighting. Trying."

The journal entry evolved into lyrical prose, my raw, unfiltered voice pouring onto the page. It was fueled by grief, exhaustion, loss of identity, transformation, uncertainty, renewal, faith, and ultimately, surrender.

In this poem, I wrestle with a truth that is often overlooked in grief. We not only mourn the person we lost, but also the person we used to be. I'd fought countless battles over twenty years. I had lived in battle mode: strong, vigilant, relentless. That's what the moments had demanded of me. But when the war ended, I was grieving both my loved ones and the identity I had carried for so long. I was mourning the physical losses, too, the remnants of a battle etched into my body. The scars of survival. The part of me I had to surrender in order to keep going.

For most of my life, I had been shaped by the roles I played. First, I was my mother's extension, fulfilling her expectations and needs. Then I became a wife, a mother, and finally a warrior, fighting for the man that I loved with everything I had. Each season of my life demanded a version of me that was defined by someone else. I knew how to battle, how to endure, how to carry burdens that were not my own.

Now, the battlefield was silent. The ones I had fought for were gone. The sword I once wielded so fiercely was no longer needed. There I stood in the aftermath, uncertain of who I was without it. If I was no longer an extension of someone, then who was I? What remained when the battles were over?

I think of how a butterfly has to fight before it can fly. Inside the cocoon, it is unmade, something unrecognizable and in order to emerge into the light and take its shape, it has to push, struggle, and press against the walls that confine it. If there was no fight, its wings would be weak and unable to carry it through the air.

Today, I see myself in that struggle. In retrospect, I see how my faith in God's name strengthened me throughout the various trials in my life, causing me to become what I needed to be in order to face each battle— even making me a warrior when it was necessary.

As I stand at the crossroads with these battles behind me, the walls of the cocoon are giving way. What beautiful butterfly will emerge? What will He cause me to become in order to make me whole?

RESTING WARRIOR

To say goodbye to you I have to let go of me
I became what was needed to get thru the war
A warrior was born
A strong, devoted, determined woman who did what was needed to get
the job done

So in reality I'm mourning the loss of two
The loss of you and the loss of the warrior woman I became to get
thru our battles.
The field of battle still has traces of smoke and scattered arrows

Smoke and scattered arrows are all that's left to see
From a blistered pavement once alive and free

Though the battle's thru, and they say I've won the war
It doesn't feel like victory when you continue to look for more

You see, the person I became in order to survive
The battle lines and valleys forged to help ease you thru
Is no longer needed, but it is clouding my view.

I'm oh so used to fighting, slaying dragons of every kind
Now that the battle's over and you're not with me any more
What's a person to do when
The warrior I've become is not needed at the fore?

I need to say goodbye to her
The woman made of steel
She did her job and got it done, now it's time to heal.
Until new battles come along needing to be waged
I'll let her rest with dignity until she's needed on the stage
Now it's time for that new life to be born
Still the same strong woman, but no longer worn

Marching through the fire transformed my gentle soul
Now what will He cause me to become in order to be whole?

THE WEIGHT
OF WHAT IF

Grief is no stranger to me. It has been a long-time companion, lingering in the corners of my life, waiting for quiet moments to make its presence known. I understand its nature, that it doesn't ask for permission, that it demands to be felt.

Even before Mark died, I knew that when grief came knocking again, I would have to meet it head-on. What I didn't know was that it would feel like guilt. In the years after his passing, a question haunted me: What if I had stayed by his side that night instead of going home? I sat with him for days as his body lingered in the space between life and death, but on that last night, my exhaustion won. I told my daughter and son-in-law that the only thing harder than losing him would be doing it without sleep. I went home, and while I slept, Mark slipped away.

I couldn't shake the feeling that I had failed him in his final moments. That my absence had changed something. That maybe, just maybe, he had been afraid, and I wasn't there to hold his hand. Logically, I knew that wasn't true, but logic and grief don't speak the same language.

For five years after Mark's death, I was numb, moving, existing, but not truly living. Grief had settled into my bones, making even the simplest things feel distant and disconnected. In the two years that followed, I began to emerge, little by little, like someone waking from a deep, dreamless sleep. And still, that one thought held me captive, the weight of "what if." If I had stayed through the night, would it have changed anything? Would it have mattered in the end?

Seven years after Mark was gone, I knew this "what if" was the last piece of the puzzle, the one thing I still had to make peace with. I joined Dr. David Kessler's bereaved spouse workshop on Zoom, a six-week course

designed to help grievers navigate the complex path of loss. I was priv-
ileged to speak with Dr. Kessler when the topic came up. He had spent
his life studying death, loss, and the stories we tell ourselves about it. He
is the world's foremost expert on grief, and what he said didn't erase the
grief, but it loosened its grip. It turned out to be one of the most healing
conversations I've ever had.

He asked me to share my most haunting "what if."

"My husband, Mark," I said, "died on April 18, 2017. He had been in
the hospital for eight days, and I stayed by his side through almost all
of it. But on that final day, I kissed him goodnight at 11 p.m. and went
home to get some sleep, and he died at 3:45 a.m."

I explained to Dr. Kessler that the guilt of not being there in his final
moments never let go of me. I'd carried it, quietly and heavily, like a
shadow tucked beneath my ribs. I still wondered if Mark's death would
have been more peaceful if I had stayed. Maybe holding his hand would
have softened something for him. Eased something. Changed something.

Dr. Kessler listened and explained that I was doing confabulation, filling
in the painful blanks with negative stories that my mind was creating.
"Do you think everyone who stays beside their spouse is guaranteed a
peaceful death?" he asked.

"No," I said.

"Do you think being there makes someone live longer?"

"No."

He spoke about a mother whose dying daughter told her, "Don't define
our entire relationship by whether you're there at the very end." That
daughter died while her mother was in the bathroom after never leaving her side for days. "Death is out of our control," he added. "When
people die is out of our control. Your husband didn't suffer because you
left. He died. The story we tell ourselves that he suffered only makes *us*
suffer more."

For me, this was a lifeline. He told me to take the truth out of my head and place it in my heart. Even if I had stayed, Mark still would have died.

My homework assignment from that workshop was to write about that night. What follows is the result of that assignment.

THE LAST DAY

Her mind says "What if"
That echoing question berates her soul
Beating her up, Beyond her control

She wants to say "shut up"
Just long enough to drown out the noise
Of that bullying voice

The woman at her core is so very kind
She's soft to a fault
Always trying to find
The answers to the questions yet unknown
What if? What then? Aren't we always alone?

In escaping the strain
She's in constant rewind
If she had stayed
Maybe he wouldn't have died?

Those endless hours between midnight and dawn
Felt like forever until he was gone
If she was there
What would have changed?
Nothing for him,
But another level to her pain

She could not suffer one more drop unseen
Chinese water torture for her
Drip, drip, drip
Like the morphine

The reality is it was easier for him
To softly slip away

Whether she stayed or not
It was his last day

Out of her control, out of her care
But never out of her heart,
He's always there
Good Night.
Sleep tight.
Sweet prince.

About a year before I took Dr. Kessler's class, I had already put some of these feelings into words, writing a poem about the nature of grief. I had started absorbing as much as I could from what I call "The Therapy of Instagram and YouTube." There had to be answers out there.

I am ever so grateful to have discovered healing tools from the therapists and coaches who pepper social media with nuggets of healing.

GRIEF

Grief is no stranger to me
The longtime companion of half a lifetime it seems

Your specific pain I do not know, nor would I ever presume to
It's like a fingerprint, so personal and unique unto you

However the companion called Grief is familiar to me
And that you have to meet it
Is something I hate to see

I have this advice, please take it from me
Lean into Grief
Let it have its say
Because if it does not speak now
It will return one day
And demand its pay

Part IV

THE BUTTERFLY

THE SEASON OF ME

Today is the first day of spring. I can smell orange blossoms in the air. The sun has lingered a little longer than before. The moon is still in the sky at sunrise as light streams into my kitchen.

Yes, *my* kitchen.

I would never have believed I'd end up living in my parents' home after they were gone. The kitchen was my mother's inner sanctum, a sacred place where she held court from a restaurant-style booth covered in brown vinyl.

Before Mark passed away, Mom gave us the primary bedroom while she moved into mine, a reversal of roles. During that first year, she commandeered my cooking, micromanaging every step. She insisted that there was only one way to do things. Her way. I acquiesced. I could tell it brought her joy. She was ninety-four and remarkably healthy.

She took pride in making her own breakfast of eggs and toast. Although she was growing frailer by the day, she assured me that she was eating enough to stay strong. She would be tickled pink any time she cracked open an egg and discovered a double yoke. I made a point to go to the Farmer's Market every week and find the biggest eggs I could, upping her odds of hitting the jackpot. It became her own little Las Vegas. Cracking the shell was like pulling the slot machine lever. When two yolks appeared, it was one of the highlights of her day.

Our house was built in 1978, and since Dad's passing in 2009, Mom hadn't done much to it, not even basic maintenance. Aside from new windows, it was all exactly the same as when we moved in, just two months before Mark passed. My mother wouldn't allow me to change a thing. "Not until I'm gone," she said. I respected her wishes, which was easy because I was too exhausted from work and caregiving to think about anything else. My artistic self had gone dormant.

After Mom passed away in July 2018, I went into overdrive. I thought I'd sell the house and downsize, but Lauren convinced me otherwise. Financially, it didn't make sense, so the first order of business was to demolish the "inner sanctum," the kitchen.

I was overwhelmed when I hung my Murano glass chandelier that Mark and I bought in Venice in 2004, in the center of my bedroom. It cast a golden glow across the soft blue walls. The champagne velvet bedding sat beneath a scrolled headboard. In the space beside the bed was a mirrored, gold-leafed dresser and nightstands with a soft image of St. Mark's Square gracing the walls. I had created what I'd been craving for decades. Peace.

FINDING THE KEY.
IDENTIFYING THE GUARDIAN

During a great deal of my life, I swallowed the glory of my achievements to make myself smaller and easier for others to accept. I hadn't been heard, and I had been punished for speaking the truth for so long, it felt like my essence had been exiled. In its place, parts of my personality had shown up with the best of intentions. They were there to protect me and help me survive, but they had become my manager. My guardian.

You better not talk too loud.

You better not say "shut up" when someone does you wrong.

You better not say no, because the price to pay is too high.

The Guardian had kept me quiet and compliant. It had stopped me from speaking my truth. The idea of keeping me safe was another word for "caged." But when I went on a "Matthew Hussey Retreat" in 2024, I learned that I didn't have to banish that part of me.

I let him go. The guardian would continue to protect me in a new role. Boundary Keeper. I stepped fully into my life at that time, and it was my first attempt at writing something other than poetry. During the week-long retreat, I was encouraged to re-focus and reframe my life, to learn how to take what I had been given and embrace it fully. I learned to live with intentionality, realizing I had the power to take the ingredients of my life and create the best gourmet meal I could imagine.

THE GUARDIAN'S FAREWELL

When I look in the mirror
And study my face
I see a young woman thru on old lady's gaze

Those grey hairs that she's earned
One tear at a time
The road map of life
Defines every line

Decisions made for her
Against her free will
She just smiled vacantly
As her spirit was slowly killed

That last day as a child stands strong in her mind
She learned that speaking her will was too high a price
So she went through the years
Quite well disguised

A Guardian born to protect that picture perfect obedient girl
He kept her silent, smiling in pearls

His job so well done for so many years
Left scars in its wake
Never vanquishing fears

Instead those walls grew in size and in stature
A guarantee that no evil force would catch her
But the joke was on her

For she failed to see
She became her own prisoner
Just trying to be

No matter which role she came to play in life's game
Be it daughter, mother or wife
She left on the alter, a sacrifice… her life
Once she had played them to an auspicious end

It became her turn to break those rules once obeyed,
Not just to bend

She made her own decisions for the very first time
To step out of those shadows she was lurking behind

She thanked her Guardian for his services rendered
And told him they were no longer needed in which to defend her
She chose to live life on her own

For the very first time
Knowing when she looks in the mirror
She leaves no stone behind.

STEPPING INTO NOW

I just turned sixty-nine years old.

For the past sixty-eight years, I've shown up consistently, lovingly, and patiently for the people in my life, whether or not they showed love in return. I've honed the skills of listening, caring, and holding space, often at the expense of my own needs.

Sometimes that neglect has resulted in self-abandonment. I've sacrificed my dreams and my desires in service of others' goals, whether they were partners, authority figures, or people with louder voices than mine.

For most of those years, I summoned the warrior inside of me. And like any warrior, my basic needs were overlooked in service of the greater good. I stayed the obedient little girl, taking care of others, even with graying hair and lines forming around my eyes.

Now those people are gone, and the lost girl who once felt so small is beginning to navigate an unfettered life with interest, curiosity, and quiet joy.

The warrior is still here, but now I see her as a guardian of Self. When future battles arise, she'll return, fierce and protective, sword at the ready. In the meantime, I have other work to do:

Tasting foods I used to gulp.

Smelling the flowers I used to rush past.

Feeling the soft hush of a gentle rain on my skin or the brush of a gentle breeze.

Recognizing joy every day.

Fully blooming in the noonday sun.

It is the season of Me.

As I begin to step into that joy without apology, an old fear is stirring quietly beneath the surface.

Can I really trust this feeling?

Can I let myself be this free?

THE PRICE OF JOY

I hope there won't be too high a price to pay
For the total and immense joy that I'm feeling

Why does it feel that a shoe must drop
Before my head stops spinning, reeling non-stop

From the pure and unadulterated love that I'm feeling
So happy and at peace
It hasn't happened in forever
At least only in my dreams

Why do I feel like my smiles will be slashed
As the price to pay for living life unabashed

The passion I feel is innocent enough
It's the zest for life that's been all but snuffed
Finally awakening from the ashes
Rekindling a familiar sort of love
A love that's full and content
With no angst or malignant intent
I'm at last embracing that lifeless part of me
That was waiting to be awakened from a very deep sleep

She's here! Alive and well
All poised for the future
A secure and happy place
In which she can dwell

Without fear of being punished
Just because of her smile
And hunger for life
Tempered for too long a while

117

Please welcome this girl
With arms open wide
She's got everything to give
With nothing to hide

She's authentic and true
Tried by life's fires
And reshaped anew

Be kind to her
This tender new shoot
Born from life's grass
From the once lifeless root

Existing is at once fragile yet strong
With tender affection
She will find where she belongs

WHERE IS THIS WRITING LEADING ME?

I've always been afraid to write. As a child, I wasn't allowed to keep a diary. You know, those sacred little books with blank pages bound by a lock and a tiny key. What power did that key hold?

A diary was forbidden. It would've been a place where I could record my own thoughts, tucked safely out of reach from the ever-watchful eye of my mother, who prided herself on knowing my every move, every feeling, every secret. God forbid I had an independent thought, or worse yet, a private one.

I was her Stepford Child. Her reflection. And my silence was her comfort.

But now, as I write, really write, I realize how powerful that little locked book truly would have been. I was right to sense that. Writing does have power. It can release decades of hidden emotions and long-buried truths. It cracks open the silence and shines light on the places where shame, guilt, and self-erasure once lived.

Writing has become my key, and that key has unlocked me. What started as journaling turned into poetry. The poetry nudged me deeper. I hired a coach, not because I wanted someone to rescue me, but because I was ready to stop letting old patterns chart my path. I began living with intentionality, curiosity, and hope.

I'm no longer deferring to a mother or a husband. There is no external voice narrating my worth. I've been given a trust. I don't mean financially, but emotionally and spiritually.

The trust to become the woman I was always meant to be.

Even now, in my 60s, I am learning.

Learning to eat alone, joyfully.

Learning to run a business.

Learning to stitch legacies into quilts, play music in a home that's finally mine, and host the kind of laughter-filled evenings I used to only dream about.

And most of all, I'm learning to love.

Not just again, but for the first time. I'm learning to love me.

I WILL FIND LOVE AGAIN

Loving another soothes the inner part of our soul
Loving another completes life's goal
Loving another is fragile yet strong
He's here one day, then poof! He's gone
The quest for love is a powerful force

It pushes or pulls us
Without any remorse

When that person is gone,
The love is not
It lives on, it's still there
Can't be sold or be bought

Trying to find a new person
Sounds tempting at first
To fill the void or escape
From feeling your worst
But now is the time for work to be done

Discover yourself, that person
Whose days have just begun
The love you try so hard to find

Isn't hard to be seen
It's there-in the mirror
And always has been

AFTERWORD

You've made it here.

Through pages laced with grief, memory, wonder, and rebuilding, through the hush of the cocoon and the whisper of wings. If you've traveled alongside me, thank you. You didn't just read my story. You held space for it, and in doing so, I hope you've held space for your own.

This isn't just a book about loss or healing. It's about becoming. About what happens when the warrior sets down her armor, not because she's defeated, but because she's found something more powerful than the fight. Peace.

The truth is, I'm still becoming. My wings are still drying. Some days, I soar. Other days, I crawl. But now I know that every stage holds beauty. Every stage belongs.

Wherever you are in your own becoming, whether you're shedding, dissolving, or stretching toward the light, I hope you carry this with you:

You are not behind.

You are not too late.

You are not alone.

There is no deadline for emergence.

If, by some miracle of timing and tenderness, these words helped you feel seen, then know this. I wrote them for you.

You are welcome in this sanctuary.

Just as you are.

Free to rest.

Free to rise.

Free to be.

✕

MY SANCTUARY

Welcome to my sanctuary,
Where dreams become reality.
It's not extraordinary—
Just life's simple things:
The sweet taste of wine,

Sunsets' glittering bling,
A drive to the coast,
Where we breathe in deep
And sink our toes in the sand,
Making memories to keep.

It's not extravagant,
But it's enough—
Because the simplest things
Bring the deepest joy
When shared with someone you dearly love.

In days gone by,
This wasn't fantasy.
These were the moments
Of everyday living.

But not anymore.
Life's become more than a chore.

So come on in.
You're warmly invited
To take refuge in my world—
Fellow warriors, united.

Here, you will not be silenced or shushed.
Your words are welcome.

They won't be hushed.
Do you even know how special you are?

Or have the people around you
Made you feel distant and small?
That won't happen here.

You are safe to be seen.
So come, peer inside—
This is my sanctuary,
Where you are free
To simply be
You.

ACKNOWLEDGEMENTS

To my editor, Andrea Cagan—with deepest gratitude for helping me shape this work from its tangled beginnings into something clear, whole, and true. You refined my words, drew out the heart of my stories, and showed me where new poems could emerge. You also gently led me to face the most daunting obstacle on my path, writing about Nancy, an act that opened a door I'd kept shut for decades. That this journey began in your workshop with Dr. David Kessler makes it feel beautifully full-circle. You helped me give these words their wings. A fitting end to a metamorphosis I never could have imagined alone.

To my publisher, Cheryl Benton —for editing with both precision and heart. You didn't just shape the work — you lifted it. And in doing so, you lifted me. Your belief in this book breathed courage into my doubts and reminded me that my lived experience could be a steadying force for others. Thank you for helping my voice rise without ever losing its truth.

The Doctors—Dr. N. – my rock, my anchor, my confidant through the darkest days. You gave me the tools to unlearn decades of enmeshment and helped me find my own voice and strength. I will forever be grateful.

Dr. Randy Scharlach, whose skilled and compassionate care helped guide Mark through his treatments and who later became my own radiation oncologist—your presence brought continuity, courage, and grace to both our journeys.

And to my own extraordinary medical team. Dr Kristi Funk, Dr. Edward Rey, Dr. Omid Shaye, Dr. Royal Dean, and Dr. Laila Malad, whose expertise and kindness carried me through my treatments with hope and healing. To Cynthia Hobbs-Hamburg, you became more than a member of my healing team, you became both a healing presence and a cheerleader. I'm so grateful for the encouragement you've continued to offer along the way.

The Coaches—Dr. David Kessler – for his classes on Bereaved Spouses, Transforming Old Wounds, and Writing Through Grief workshops, and for helping me navigate the river of grief.

Dr. Sue M. - Your gentle wisdom and insight helped me make peace with some of the deepest wounds I carried. Your voice still echoes in the quiet places where I pause to reflect.

Mr. Jonathon Aslay – whose coaching helped me take the first brave steps on the path of self-discovery.

Mr. Matthew Hussy and the 2024 Retreat Team – for stripping down the stories we tell ourselves, for identifying the Guardian within, and begin the work of giving it a new role. Your teachings continue to echo in my journey.

The Wind Beneath My Wings—Erik and Lauren Scott—for your unwavering love, patience, and encouragement as I brought this book to life. You didn't just support the process — you walked through the fire with me. Erik, your steady presence through Mark's illness, and the phrase you coined— *sustaining the unsustainable*—captured what so much of that season felt like. And Lauren, though the dedication bears your name, this acknowledgment is my way of saying it again: thank you. For showing up, for holding space, and for helping me find the strength to tell it all.

To Mr. Colin Salter — Thank you for the music that crossed my path when I wasn't seeking anything at all. More than an amazingly talented entertainer and performer, your gift for turning back the clock to happier times floods the room— and makes us *"forget about life for a while."*

I am forever grateful.

The Nancy Core— who despite carrying their own grief stood strong and helped support all of us along the way.

To the ones who stayed —

who stood in the quiet,

who held the weight without needing to be asked —

you weren't just part of the journey,

you were the lifelines that made it possible.

To the trusted guide who stood quietly beside me, offering encouragement, wisdom, and strength when I needed it most. Thank you for believing in me.

But most of all, to my God, Jehovah—Who Causes to Become.

ABOUT THE AUTHOR

Ruthie Chamichian-Smith is a real estate professional, quilt artisan, and lifelong seeker of understanding. With a deep curiosity about why we are the way we are—and how we heal, grow, and connect—she has long explored the inner workings of the mind and heart. Writing her first book, *Resting Warrior*, became an unexpected but natural extension of this lifelong pursuit. Through personal stories and poetry, she reflects on themes of transformation, grief, resilience, and hope—offering hard-won insights shaped by love, loss, and the courage to begin again. When she isn't writing or quilting, Ruthie enjoys music, traveling, and keeping cherished family recipes alive for those she loves. She lives in Southern California with her beloved Maltese, Bianca.

THE MUSIC
BY MY SIDE

Music had been missing from my life for a long time. Reclaiming it, song by song, became part of my healing and part of this journey.

The songs on this playlist reflect the very journey of metamorphosis I've written about: some echo the yearning of the caterpillar, some speak to the stillness and uncertainty of the chrysalis, others to the struggle of breaking free—and many to the wonder of emerging.

Some of these songs have been with me since I was a little girl; two of them I reference in these pages; others became trusted companions along the way. Together, they were the music by my side. I hope they might be by yours, too – wherever you are on your own path of becoming.

Scan to listen on Spotify.